WHEN OLD SCHOOL MEETS NEW SCHOOL

Keys for Bridging the Gap of Respect

Lestie May Zachary

To Dad and Mom for shaping my young mind with the example set by living a respect-filled life.

To my grandchildren and future greats: Create your ripple effect of love and light through 'Kindness in Motion.'
Make it boundless and infinite.

Thank you to my family and friends for their support and to my mentors and collaborators for helping bring this book to life.

Publisher's Cataloging-in-Publication data

Names: Zachary, Lestie May, author.
Title: When old school meets new school : 7 keys for bridging the gap of respect / Lestie May Zachary.
Description: Horseshoe Bend, AR: Lestie May Zachary, 2023. | Summary: Guidebook with stories, lessons, & activities that help kids 11-14 years of age learn how to be more respectful.

Identifiers: LCCN: 2023905469 | ISBN: 979-8-9880580-5-2 (paperback) | 979-8-9880580-1-4 (ebook) | 979-8-9880580-2-1 (coil bound) | 979-8-9880580-3-8 (audio)

Subjects: LCSH Respect--Juvenile literature. | Preteens--Conduct of life--Juvenile literature. | Teenagers--Conduct of life--Juvenile literature. | Character--Juvenile literature. | Family--Juvenile literature. | Christian life--Biblical teaching--Juvenile literature. | Conduct of life. | BISAC JUVENILE NONFICTION / Family / Multigenerational | JUVENILE NONFICTION / Religious / Christian / Family & Relationships | JUVENILE NONFICTION / Religious / Christian / Inspirational | JUVENILE NONFICTION / Religious / Christian / Values & Virtues

Classification: LCC BJ1631 .Z33 2023| DDC 248.8/2--dc23

Lestie Zachary is a veteran homeschooling teacher with years of experience.
A Southwest USA native, she loves to write about her family roots. When she's not writing or doting on family, she and her husband enjoy the cabin life on Crown Lake in Horseshoe Bend, Arkansas.

Everyone loves a
FREEBIE

Scan this QR code for a special gift from the author.

For More Info Visit:

Instagram: @lmzpublishing
Facebook: Facebook.com/lmzpublishing
Email: lestie@lestiemayzachary.com
www.lestiemayzachary.com

WHAT'S INSIDE

Introduction

Have you ever heard of 'the ripple effect'? You see it when you throw a stone into a pond or lake. The impact of the falling stone creates waves around it that ripple outward. If you apply the same idea to social settings, that rock would be YOU. It means that whenever you speak, listen, or act, you're creating ripples with big and small impacts.

In 2009, my oldest nephew, Justin, was killed in a car accident while texting and driving. It happened just before his eighteenth birthday. The ripple effects he created by choosing to text while driving turned out to be life-altering for him—and our whole family.

At our family reunion a year later, we gathered in a big circle before the meal to honor Justin by recalling a few stories as we stood united in grief. After some recollections were shared, my sister-in-law Cindy felt that the almost unbearable weight of the moment needed to shift. In her soft-spoken voice, she slowly and cautiously began to sing: "*You put your right foot in—You take your right foot out.*" We all felt as if a pressure valve had been released.

We laughed as we all joined in with the playful movements that go along with the words of the sing-song tune, 'Hokey Pokey.' Our spirits lifted with the lightness of the scene as we made the motions of "turning ourselves around." Cindy didn't realize that she'd created a ripple effect that day. The ripples were powerful ones of love and connection that lightened the sadness of our family.

So, tell me. Do you consider yourself respectful to friends, family, teachers—and even to yourself? If YOU were the rock thrown into the lake, would your respectful approach be enough to create a widespread ripple? Or would it be like tossing a tiny grain of sand into the lake, barely moving the water at all?

Here's the good news: The chapters of this book can effectively guide the ways you learn about respect. Even if you feel like the most disrespectful person in the world, with this guided study, you will gain the knowledge and tools you'll need to become your best self.

You might be thinking, "*Ugh!* All of that sounds boring." But I assure you, I have created a uniquely original and interactive way for you to grasp some great concepts without yawning even once! You'll be drawn into the stories and activities in every lesson—like word searches, scrambles, and code-breaking. And with every key, you'll have a quiz that you can use to find out just how respectful you are. In the end, you'll be able to add up your scores to discover your overall level of respectfulness. You're likely to have as much fun with all these activities as I did creating them for you!

So, let's make some ripples.

Are you ready?
Get set...and...GO!

Dad and our little red Volkswagon

WISDOM

> " Life is a succession of lessons which must be lived to be understood. "
>
> Helen Keller

WISDOM

Riding With Dad

The dinky red 1960s Volkswagen Beetle *puttered* up the dirt road toward the Florida Mountains. We were traveling just outside the city of Deming, in Southwest New Mexico: The flat-landed town of my birth. Dad, Mom, my four-year-old brother, and I, a little three-year-old, were out for an evening drive. The jagged formation of this mountain range is an imposing sight from town. But it was even more intimidating while beginning the ride upward. It was late afternoon when we ventured out on our scenic drive. We rambled through the changing landscape from the desert floor to the steep canyons and vertical cliffs. As we climbed ever higher, the lights of the town below us started to glow as the sun was setting.

The view from my window was scary. The road's edge wasn't visible, but I could see thousands of feet below with absolute clarity. An unease crept into my tiny tummy. I decided right then that I did not like this ride *one bit*. I gripped the grab handle so tightly—desperately trying to prevent us from crashing down the mountainside. My panic intensified as Dad pulled off at a lookout point. My overactive imagination believed he was going to drive right over the cliff.

"Daddy, *STOP*! We're gonna fall off!" My little trembling lips and chin could not hold back the tears that began to flow.

Unruffled by the anguish overflowing from me in the back seat, Dad burst out laughing! He had a great sense of humor. But I didn't see anything funny about our impending doom. Of course, we were never in any real danger. Dad was a good driver. He had only thought we'd enjoy seeing the lights of town from the mountainside.

"Well, now, Little One. It's okay," Dad said. "We're not going to fall off. I won't let that happen," he promised with great assurance. After my trembling had subsided and I'd wiped away my tears, I figured what Dad told me had to be true. He wouldn't put us in danger.

Fast-forward five years.

"Dad, can I go with you to the mailbox?" We were at my grandparents' cotton farm, where Mom and her sister had spent their formative years. It was about a half-mile drive on the dirt road from the farmhouse to the mailbox at Waterloo Road.

"Can I drive, *pleeease*?" I begged. On the few occasions when I got to drive before that day, it had been while sitting in my dad's lap. As we jumped into our new 1973 Ford pickup truck, Dad thoughtfully answered, "We'll see." I sat beside Dad, excited and eager. I imagined driving the car back to the adobe farmhouse while in the driver's seat.

Dad got out of the truck to get the mail. I asked again, "Can I drive home?" When Dad replied, "Yes," I quickly scooted over into the driver's seat, put the truck in drive, and started to pull away—leaving Dad at the mailbox. *It's a short walk home*, I thought. *Surely he'll meet me there soon.*

"*Hey*!" Dad hollered. "*STOP*! Put your foot on the brake!" He started running toward the truck. Thankfully, I had 'driven' enough to be familiar with the brake's function. I brought the vehicle to a quick halt after it had rolled forward a couple of car lengths. Breathless and scared, Dad reached over me and put the truck in park, exclaiming,
"What the hell were you thinking?"

"You said I could drive back," I answered. Then, I suddenly realized my error in judgment. Dad asked me, "How did you think I would get back to the house?" To me, his fright sounded like anger.

"You could have been hurt, Lestie!" My trembling legs displayed the fear that was enveloping my body. Would I get a spanking? What if I had wrecked Dad's new truck? Suddenly, I felt so embarrassed that I started to cry.

Dad's silence spoke volumes. The short ride home seemed like the longest half-mile of my life. Though I was rattled, I was thankful for Dad's quiet demeanor. It gave me time to think about the danger I'd caused with my actions. Lesson learned: I never pulled that stunt again.

Fast-forward another five years.

I found myself riding with Dad through the Prescott National Forest. We drove this route occasionally through the Mingus Mountain region of central Arizona. The stunning vistas from the top always leave a person longing for more. Though the elevation was similar to the Florida mountain range, the landscape was very different.

While the Florida's mountains had scrub brush, mesquite, and juniper trees, it was the scents of the Mingus in Arizona that became firmly imprinted in my memory: Lovely aromas of the abundant vanilla pines, elderberry bushes, and prickly pear cactus.

Since that nail-biting trip through the Florida Mountains as a three-year-old, I had grown in many ways-but Dad still had his fun-loving, mischievous sense of humor. He never lost an opportunity to test my nerve as we wound our way over the mountain. Dad would inch ever closer to the guardrails at some of the highest peaks, grinning at me, waiting for a reaction. Half smiling back at him, I'd exclaim, "Dad, don't! You know how that gets me." Acting like he couldn't turn the steering wheel fast enough to prevent a wreck, he'd answer, "What? This?" And he'd get a good chuckle from my nervous reaction.
Dad often enjoyed 'getting a rise out of me.'

Yet, throughout those few years, I learned to trust this man with my life, never doubting how much he loved me. While I was riding with Dad, he would continue to stretch my educational and emotional limits where confidence was concerned. I experienced the thrill and the dangers that vehicles posed. I also learned that with a keen sense of humor, I could take life just a little less seriously and enjoy the small adventures that came my way.

DAY 1

Observe Before Taking Action

The title of today's lesson is "Observe Before Taking Action." Of the three stories in "Riding with Dad," which one of these summaries best fits today's lesson?

1. Being afraid of falling off the cliff, or
2. My driving without Dad in the truck, or
3. Dad driving near the guardrails of the Mingas Mountain roads?

If you chose #2, you're a 'smart cookie!'

Do you think I considered how Dad would get back to the house from the mailbox?

Yes or No?

Do you think I considered my safety before putting the truck in motion?

Yes or No?

Do you think I thought about Dad's truck and what would happen if I wrecked it?

Yes or No?

The truth is, I didn't think about anything except getting in the driver's seat and having the thrill of getting the chance to drive. I was so excited about this rare opportunity that I threw caution and common sense to the wind. I assumed Dad would walk back to the house. I took action absentmindedly before observing my surroundings, didn't I?

Let's consider what I could have done differently while driving with Dad. Below, write what you think would have been the wise thing to do after Dad told me I could drive the truck.

_____

_____

Color the picture below. As you do, be mindful as you consider ways that a person should observe their surroundings before taking action.

DAY 2

Use Your Voice Wisely

Gaining wisdom takes careful thought. Consider your actions and how they will affect others around you before you become involved. It's a wise move to carefully observe your surroundings before taking action. It shows respect and consideration.

The same goes for speaking out of turn. Have you ever walked up to a group of friends holding a conversation and blurted out something pointless or irrelevant to the subject matter?

Proverbs 13:3 NIV says, "Those who guard their lips preserve their lives, but those who speak rashly will come to ruin." A respectful and respectable person is careful to speak without interrupting. Always believe that what others have to say is just as important as your own input.

Do you find yourself butting into conversations with your friends? Yes or No?

Consider the conversations you had the last time you were with your friends. What is *one thing* you could have done or said differently to show consideration for what they had to say?

_____

_____

Is it wiser to be heard-or know when to speak? Why?

_____

Turn This Scene Around

You've just shared a rumor that's not true with a group of your friends. When you told it, you knew it was likely untrue. But you laughed with your friends anyway, further hurting the person you gossiped about.

Now, when I snap my finger, you'll have a complete turnaround of thought. You realize you handled that scene poorly. What would you do differently this time? Explain below.
Ready....and...

_____

_____

_____

WISDOM SCRAMBLE

Unscramble the words in the first row by connecting them with their match on the right.

VEERSBO ●	● LISTEN
STILEN ●	● REFLECT
CUEDETA ●	● EDUCATE
CVIEAD ●	● TRUTH
LERFTEC ●	● KNOWLEDGE
UTTHR ●	● OBSERVE
WEDNGLEKO ●	● ADVICE

DAY 3

Take Direction

When my nephew, Justin, was taken from us in that fateful car accident in 2009, we started finding what's described in the Scripture *Jeremiah 29:11* ESV appearing everywhere around us: "For I know the plans I have for you, declares the Lord, plans for welfare and not for evil, to give you a future and a hope." We'd see it in places like greeting cards, notice it in sermons, and even hear it in radio announcements. We soon realized this frequent reminder was from God—specifically a Scripture for our family.

When tragedy strikes, it's difficult to understand God's ways. People often blame Him for life's hardships. But the words: "plans," "not for evil," "future," and "hope" gave us a Truth we could hold onto.

True wisdom comes when we take direction from the Holy Spirit. You might ask, "But how can I take direction if I can't even hear Him?" That's a great question—and one many people grapple with. One important thing about the Holy Spirit is that He is omniscient—which is a big word and an even bigger idea. It means His knowledge is limitless. Father God knows every single detail about you. It's pretty mind-blowing, right? So, if He knows you so personally, wouldn't He be able to speak to you in ways you could understand? You *betcha'* He could. And he does. ALL. THE. TIME.

Can you think of a time when you thought you could sense God trying to tell you something? If you answered yes: What did you hear, and what did you do with that information?

_____

_____

_____

_____

If your answer is no, you're not alone. It takes time to learn how to hear that still, small voice of the Lord. But thankfully, He is patient and committed to connecting with you. Today, find a quiet, comfortable place to sit. Calm your mind. Ask a question like this: "Holy Spirit, what would You like me to know today?" He takes your requests seriously. It will most likely give you an *"ah-ha"* moment or confirm what you already know to be true when He speaks. Write what you hear below. If you don't hear anything, ask a different question. Give the Holy Spirit space and time to answer. Continue this practice daily. Keep journal notes about the things you discover. You'll be amazed at what you hear!

_____

_____

WISDOM

WORD SEARCH

```
K  Z  R  A  F  D  F  R  M  E  U  J
E  P  E  R  C  E  P  T  I  V  E  M
Y  T  A  C  S  B  I  N  C  I  O  H
F  B  S  S  T  L  D  X  U  T  E  R
O  F  O  N  R  W  N  L  Z  C  P  E
R  L  N  X  O  Y  A  Q  D  E  D  A
E  A  T  Z  K  C  T  P  O  P  R  V
S  T  S  C  I  O  S  B  G  S  H  E
I  W  J  G  E  A  R  H  D  O  Z  I
G  A  O  T  R  S  E  F  J  R  M  A
H  L  L  G  N  W  D  P  F  T  W  O
T  C  O  M  M  O  N  S  E  N  S  E
Q  W  A  F  Y  R  U  E  S  I  W  J
```

FORESIGHT	UNDERSTAND	INTROSPECTIVE
COMMON SENSE	WISE	REASON
LOGICAL	GRASP	PERCEPTIVE

DAY 4

Ask For Advice

Author Roy T. Bennett said, "Remember that things are not always as they appear to be... Curiosity creates possibilities and opportunities."

Each morning, you awaken refreshed to a day full of opportunities to learn something new. Take a minute to think about three things you are curious about learning. Fire up your imagination! Write them below.

1._____ 2._____ 3._____

When you learn something new, asking for advice is wise. Chances are, you have parents, grandparents, or mentors who can teach you ways to achieve your goals. If you happen to know who is knowledgeable about the thing you want to learn, by all means, ask them. Don't be shy about asking. We all learn from one another. That's how you gain wisdom.

The Scripture in *Proverbs 4:13* MSG says, "Hold tight to good advice; don't relax your grip. Guard it well-your life is at stake!" You can't gain wisdom if you are not willing to seek advice. When Jesus walked this Earth, men, women, and children sought after his teaching. He told us that God is generous to share His wisdom with us. I always find that I could use more knowledge. How about you?

Opposites

Draw a line between the left-hand and right-hand columns connecting
the wisdom word with its opposite. Use a thesaurus if you'd like.

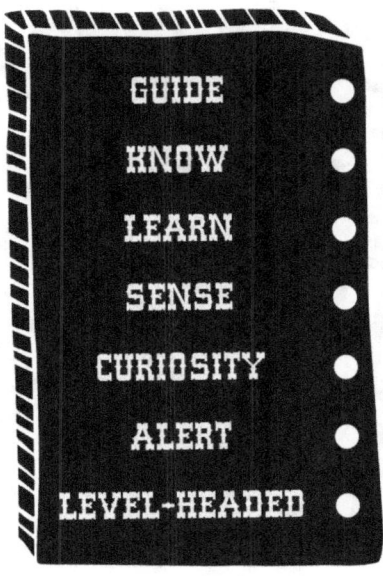

GUIDE
KNOW
LEARN
SENSE
CURIOSITY
ALERT
LEVEL-HEADED

MISUNDERSTAND
CARELESS
DISINTEREST
FORGET
ANGST
FOOLISHNESS
MISLEAD

WISDOM MAZE

Help KIM reach the key to wisdom.
Keep track of how many keys KIM has collected on page 125....

DAY 5

Educate Yourself

Education most likely will mean stepping out of your comfort zone. I think back to Dad driving a little too close to the road's edge for my comfort. The scene looked much different as a teenager than when I was three years old. Expanding my knowledge over the years helped me understand that Dad was a safe driver. His plan did not include flying off the cliff but arriving safely at our destination.

Observation is one of many ways to educate yourself. One essential thing to remember is that knowledge is a powerful tool. When you branch out to learn something new, you increase your ability to understand with greater clarity and mastery. Your confidence is sure to grow as you take on each unique experience.

A well-known passage of scripture you may have heard gives this timeless advice that applies to all of us: "Don't become so well-adjusted to your culture that you fit into it without even thinking. Instead, fix your attention on God. You'll be changed from the inside out. Readily recognize what He wants from you, and quickly respond to it. Unlike the culture around you, always dragging you down to its level of immaturity, God brings the best out of you, developing well-formed maturity in you" (*Romans 12:2* MSG).

Check the True or False box for each statement.

	T	F
Asking advice is for the weak-minded.	☐	☐
Wisdom is developed over time.	☐	☐
Wisdom is foolishness.	☐	☐
A desire to learn assures you won't be easily bored.	☐	☐
Ignoring a wise person is thoughtless.	☐	☐
Knowledge is a powerful tool.	☐	☐
You have all the wisdom you need at the age of 18.	☐	☐

WISDOM
Code Breaker

Use the key below to break the code.

A	B	C	D	E	F	G	H	I	J	K	L	M
🥾	🌱	🐄	♥	💡	👢	✈	🔫	👥	📖	👨‍👦	💕	⛺

N	O	P	Q	R	S	T	U	V	W	X	Y	Z
🚗	🤠	🌲	✓	🏇	🚙	♡	🤝	🔑	💟	⛰	🕯	➰

"

HOW MUCH BETTER

TO GET WISDOM

THAN GOLD, TO GET

INSIGHT RATHER

THAN SILVER. "

14

DAY 6

Be Introspective

According to the internet, an individual has anywhere from two thousand one hundred to eighty thousand thoughts per day. That's a whole lot of thinking going on! Don't you agree? Consider the thoughts in your head. On average, would you say your thoughts are mostly *Positive* *Negative* *Selfish* *Empathetic* *Self-doubting* *Loving*? Circle the kind of thoughts that apply. Are you surprised by your answers? _____
Why or why not? _____
There are no incorrect or correct answers to these questions. This exercise gets you to think about being introspective, which means looking within. When you look in a mirror, you see your outer reflection. But what is revealed when you look inward? Do you see the person you want to become? You are fully capable of intentional thinking. Simply put: *You are what you think.* When you look inward thoughtfully, you are becoming introspective.

Did you know God created your unique and brilliant brain to do good
things—and even extraordinary ones—in your lifetime?

"For everything created by God is good, and nothing is to be rejected if it is received with thanksgiving" (*1 Timothy 4:4* ESV).

REFLECTION TIME

Apathy is the opposite of introspection. Apathy is the absence of concern, and it's a behavior we all must correct. When we seek the benefit of others through our thoughts and actions, we become images of God's love. Answer the questions below.

How does it make you feel when you hear news of war?
Helpless? ____ Sad? ____ Worried? ____ Angry? __ Don't care? __
If you had the power to stop it, what would you do?

_____

How does it make you feel when you hear about a natural disaster that devastated a community? Helpless? __ Sad? __ Worried? __ Angry? __ Don't care? __
If you could help this community, what would you do?

_____

_____

Think of a friend. If you could change a bad situation in their life into a hopeful one, how might you go about it? _____

WISDOM
Self Evaluation Worksheet

Check the boxes that are true for you.

I can...	I can do this very well	I can do this fairly well	I can do this with some help	I need more practice
Observe before taking action				
Use my voice wisely				
Take direction				
Ask for advice				
Educate myself				
Be introspective				

Complete the table below.

I can gain wisdom by	
One thing I need to improve	
To improve I can	
One thing I'd like to learn this year	

DAY 7

Embrace Truth

Does it feel like you're growing up in a confusing time? The television news that's supposed to be objective has conflicting stories. And I'm sure you hear things at school or on the internet that make you question the truth. Sometimes it's hard to know.

So, how do you know who-or what-to believe?

Guideline #1

The first place to go to try to make sense of the unknown is God. The book of *Proverbs 30:5* ERV tells us, "You can trust this: Every word that God speaks is true. God is a safe place for those who go to Him." Then in *John 16:13* ESV, Jesus speaks to his disciples, saying, "When the Spirit of Truth comes, he will guide you into all the Truth, for He will not speak on His own authority, but whatever He hears He will speak, and He will declare to you the things that are to come." We've talked before about finding quiet time with God. Bring your questions before Him. Listen carefully for the answer.

Guideline #2

Another way to help you determine the truth is to seek wise mentors for your questions. These should include your parents, grandparents, uncles, aunts, church leaders, foster parents, and teachers. This is how *1 Thessalonians 5:21-22* NLT instructs us: "But test everything that is said. Hold on to what is good. Stay away from every kind of evil." You will gain wisdom when you put these words to the test.

In basketball, only one ball goes through the hoop at a time, right? Every basket that you make will award you points. Wisdom is similar in that you don't gain a lifetime of wisdom with only one shot. It takes experience and knowledge to gain each point.

We've spent a whole week learning about wisdom. Now it's time to put your knowledge to the test. Turn the page to find the WISDOM QUIZ. Answer each question to the best of your ability. Then turn the page over to calculate your score. There will be a quiz after the completion of each key. After the seventh key, you will tally your scores to determine your level of respectfulness.

Now, GO FORTH AND TAKE YOUR BEST SHOT!

WISDOM KEY

How wise are you? Circle the best answer for each scenario.

1. You've never smoked before, but your friend asks you to try one. Do you...

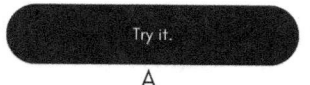

Try it.	Say, "You're stupid for smoking."	Say, "Maybe later" to avoid get teased.	Encourage your friend not to smoke.
A	B	C	D

2. The popular guy brought alcohol to school. He asks you to drink it with him. Do you...

Encourage your friends to try it first.	Kindly say, "No thank you."	Drink it to avoid getting teased.	Make fun of him.
A	B	C	D

3. Your neighbor paid you for mowing her lawn but gave you too much. Do you...

Take it and say, "Thank you."	Ask, "Did you mean to give me that much?"	Justify your need for the extra and don't say anything.	Pretend she didn't overpay you.
A	B	C	D

4. Your classmate is misbehaving and not listening to the teacher. Do you...

Join him in misbehaving.	Let the teacher handle it.	Encourage your classmate to listen to the teacher.	Laugh, causing more raucous.
A	B	C	D

5. You have to study for a test, but your friend wants to hang out longer. Do you...

Say, "Yeah. Why not?"	Go home and study.	Go home but delay studying.	Figure you'll pass the test without studying.
A	B	C	D

6. A bunch of your friends plan to climb the city water tower illegally. Do you...

Choose not to participate.	Feel scared, but are willing to try it.	Go but not climb.	Get to the top first.
A	B	C	D

Talk about your answers with a parent, grandparent, or mentor.

WISDOM
QUIZ KEY

On the Wisdom quiz page, you circled A, B, C or D for each scenario.

You can see below that each letter is = to a number from 0 to 3

In the 'Points' box, write the number = to the letter
you circled for each scenario in the quiz.

Next, add the numbers together at the bottom for your total.

1. A=0 B=1 C=2 D=3

2. A=1 B=3 C=0 D=2

3. A=2 B=3 C=1 D=0

4. A=0 B=2 C=3 D=1

5. A=1 B=3 C=2 D=0

6. A=3 B=1 C=2 D=0

Points

+ _____

Next, write your total from this page in the Wisdom
box on page 123 to calculate your overall score.

Total

HONOR

Dad, loving the great outdoors

Wiggins Crossing Camp Site

> It is not the honor that you take with you, but the heritage you leave behind.
>
> Branch Rickey

HONOR

Camping With Dad

One of the most cherished memories of my dad was Labor Day weekend, circa 1976. Three-day weekends were perfect for camping getaways. Wiggins Crossing was the go-to spot in our youth.

The five of us and our Doberman dog, Heidi, struck out at 4:00 a.m., Saturday morning. Mom had made sausage biscuits for the road trip the night before. The green fiberglass trailer was stocked with bedrolls, well-conditioned tarps, water jugs, and the food we would consume that weekend. We were not the typical campers you'd see at the campground. *No, siree*. We roughed it. There were no bathrooms. And there was no one to see or hear for miles around. Dad had a knack for finding the perfect spot, untouched by human traffic.

We were set to unload our supplies. Mom began setting up her kitchen. Dad laid out the tarps, using the trailer as a makeshift tent for us girls. Dad was a master of knots. When he tied a knot, it stayed secure until we were ready to break down our camp. But even at break down time, I had a hard time loosening Dad's knots. He said, "Here, let me show you a little trick." He held the rope in both hands and did what appeared to be a sleight of hand movement. I took the rope into my hands, attempting the same knot Dad had just tied with ease. I looked more like a walrus trying to knit. It was a skill to be learned, and Dad had plenty of patience to teach me.

The three of us kids were sent out to gather firewood. "Keep your eyes peeled for bears," Dad warned. He got our attention with that! My sister, Megan, called out, "Come on, Heidi," assuming the dog would ward off unwanted intruders. My brother, Brandt, loaded my sister's arms and mine with as much firewood as we could carry in one load. He dragged in a weightier branch that had fallen. We dropped off our load near the spot Mom had prepared for the fire.

"*Ouch*," I complained. "I got a splinter in my finger. Dad, can you get it out?" He was the best 'splinter taker-outer' in the West. He reached into his pocket to pull out his handy-dandy pocket knife as I walked toward him. One might be wary of walking toward a man holding a knife, but I knew well that he was gentle and always knew the right angle to hold the knife for removing a splinter. That time, Dad said, "There it is. No bigger than the eye of a needle." He rubbed over my finger where the irritant had been removed. I was not a fan of bugs, snakes, dirt, or splinters. But Dad knew just the right thing to say to calm me down.

"Brandt B., why don't you grab the shovel and dig us a hole for the roast?" Dad suggested. "We need to get it started if we want supper tonight." Dad motioned toward the tree where the ax, rake, and shovel leaned. The meats we cooked in an underground pit rivaled the best-flavored of any recipes in the country.

Mom seasoned the roast with her secret recipe rub, then wrapped it securely in aluminum foil to prevent leakage—or infiltration of wood ash. Then, she put the roast in a gunny sack soaked with water. This prevented the meat from drying out while cooking in the pit. Dad assisted Brandt in getting the campfire blazing. We needed good hot coals to transfer to the hole to cook the roast.

Megan played with Heidi while I helped Mom get lunch ready: A simple sandwich, Mom's homemade sweet pickles, and potato chips. It seems like we kids were always wanting to nibble on something. Mom had made trail mix the day before we came out to camp. Our tastebuds agreed the snack was delicious!

After the lunch fixings were put away and the trash cleared, I ambled away from camp with my pen and notebook. I loved these times in the forest! The smell of the pines with the cool breeze filtering through them was heavenly. The leaves and pine needles on the ground crunched beneath my feet. I sat upon a fallen log, listening to all the sounds around me. The freedom to write was mine. 'The world was my oyster!'

I returned to camp just in time to watch Dad move the coals to the pit. Knowing just how long to keep the roast buried seemed like an art form. Brandt had dug the hole about a foot into the ground earlier, as Dad had instructed. Doing that created plenty of space to add the coals on the bottom, around, and on top of the roast. Then, Dad shoveled dirt over the top of the pit to seal in the heat.

Dad invited us, "Come on, kids. Let's go for a walk." Brandt, Megan, and I hightailed it to catch up. We did not hesitate. Dad had a way of commanding respect without being overbearing. Camping together was not only fun but a learning experience, too. We had walked a fair distance when Dad finally stopped and spoke: "See the moss on this side of the tree and the other trees around?" All three of us chimed in, "Yes, sir."

"If you ever get lost, you can always figure out in which direction you're going. Do you know in which direction the moss is facing?" I piped up, "East?" Brandt snickered at me like Muttley, the cartoon dog. Dad smiled and said, "The moss will always grow on the north side because that side gets less sun. The snow will also melt last on the north side."

We continued our hike, descending a steep hillside. Dad instructed, "Be sure of your footing. When you step on a rock, test it before putting your full weight on it. Walk in the clearing, if possible, to avoid slipping on the pine needles."

I was winded by this point, so my breathing and steps were heavy. Dad stopped and said, "Walk lightly. If we were hunting, you would have scared off the game." I suddenly realized how noisy we were—tromping along the forest floor.

Dad had an ulterior motive for leading us away from camp for our hike. He asked us, "Which way is it back to camp? Lead the way."

Trying to remember our steps backward was more challenging than you'd think. We were solely reliant on Dad being Dad to get us back safely. We landed west of camp, but the campfire and the aroma of Mom prepping the side dishes for the roast brought us around full circle.

The roast and skillet-cooked potatoes, carrots, and onions were delicious. Food always tasted better cooked on a campfire. We told Mom all about our exploits on the hike. She smiled at Dad as we carried on.

The sun sank low on the horizon. We completed our last-minute preparations for bedding down. Then Dad drew us back to the fire with his guitar picking. He played the old familiar favorites, and we sang along. We enjoyed the great outdoors that summer for two more days with Dad as our lead man. You know, honor doesn't always come with a medal. Sometimes, honor comes in the form of giving of yourself to help others grow into their best potential.

DAY 1

Honor God

Let's do a heart check. Put your hand over your heart.

Feel it beating? That rhythm is a sign of life: A life designed to honor God. The bible speaks specifically that God sought out David, son of Jesse, because he was a man after God's own heart. I like the verse in which God says of David, "He's a man whose heart beats to my heart, a man who will do what I tell him" (*Acts 13:22b* MSG).

The most valuable commission we have, according to *Matthew 22:37b* ESV, is this: "You shall love the Lord your God with all your heart and with all your soul and with all your mind." These three powers within us represent our whole being. We can use these powers for good or bad. We honor God and others when we use these powers for good. He has given us the Holy Spirit to help direct our paths, but He lets us decide which direction to take. When we make honorable decisions by radiating love to others and even ourselves, He is well pleased.

Let's think of ways we can use these powers for good. I'll start. I'll name three examples. Then you list as many ways as you can think of to honor God.

Love God with your whole heart, soul, and mind.
Look for ways to help others..
Respect your elders.

_____
_____

Color the picture below. As you do, be mindful as you consider ways you can be honorable.

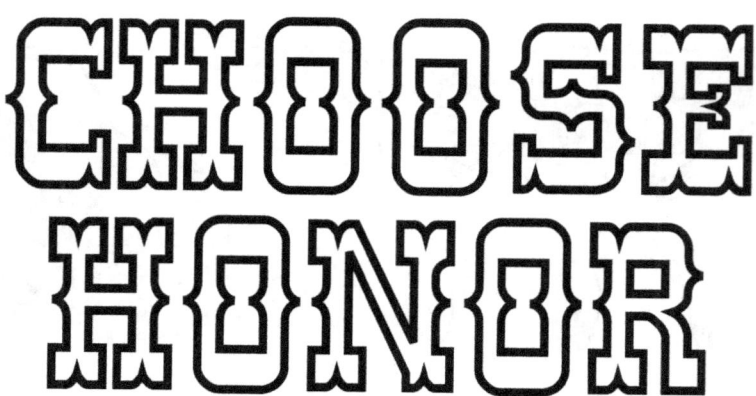

DAY 2

Obey Your Parents

We kids didn't know at the time, but the lessons Dad taught in the 'Camping with Dad' story were life skills we would use from then on. You see, even in everyday life, we extend our knowledge by following the examples set by our parents, grandparents, guardians, and mentors.

We also have a common-sense guide in the Holy Bible to help us understand this relationship more fully. It's called the Ten Commandments. You may have heard of these rules the Israelites were given as a guide for daily living. The fifth one specifically deals with the child and parent relationship, "Honor your father and your mother, that your days may be long in the land that the Lord your God is giving you" (*Exodus 20:12* ESV). This commandment is wise counsel because your parents have at least one generation's-worth of wisdom to their credit to train you in the way you should go. The same applies here to grandparents, guardians, and mentors. When you listen and observe, you honor those who teach you.

Mention one valuable lesson you've learned so far from your parents (include grandparents, guardians, and mentors if you'd like).

_____
_____
_____

Turn This Scene Around

You are mad at your mom for making you stay home and do chores instead of allowing you to go out with your friends. You slam things around in your bedroom to show your anger. Your attitude needs an adjustment, *pronto*.

Now, when I snap my finger, your attitude changes from one of anger to respect. How does your attitude look now? Explain below. Ready...and...

_____
_____
_____

HONOR SCRAMBLE

Unscramble the words in the first row by connecting them with their match on the right.

TABUEERPL	OBJECTIVE
LOMAR	PRINCIPLE
YONSTEH	RESPECTFUL
PLCINIREP	MORAL
TEVECOBIJ	REPUTABLE
SULPECETFR	HONESTY
GETTIYRIN	INTEGRITY

DAY 3

Be Trustworthy

My Uncle David, Dad's brother, recalled a great example of lesson in a short story:

The principal at the Hachita School noticed the oldest May boy, now in junior high school, showing off a new twenty-dollar bill to his friends. That was a lot of money in the mid-1950s. So, the principal called to report this to Grandpa but he didn't say anything to Dad. When the school bus stopped at the drop-off point, Grandpa waved and said, "Hop in! We need to go check the water at the Jarrel headquarters." He was talking about the ranch where he worked. On the way, Grandpa inquired, "Buris, a twenty-dollar bill is missing from the station drawer. Do you know anything about that?"

"*No sir*!" was his quick reply. After he denied knowing anything about the twenty dollars, Dad felt sick to his stomach. Not only had he taken the money, but he'd also lied to his father. His own deception overwhelmed him. So, when he got out to open a gate at the ranch, he slipped the twenty dollars out of his pocket, onto the ground, and into the wind. They were almost back to the house when Grandpa said, "Buris, if you say you didn't take that money, I believe you. I trust you." That was too heavy for my dad. He broke down and cried and said, "I'm sorry! I did take it." When Grandpa asked him where it was, Dad said, "I threw it away at the gate." Turning the pickup around, they headed back up the county road. Incredibly, the twenty-dollar bill had blown against the barbed wire fence and was hanging out there until they returned. Grandpa never brought the subject up ever again. There was no condemnation—no lack of trust! It made a powerful impression on my dad: A young man who loved and revered his father.

God corrects us in much the same way Grandpa taught Dad that life lesson with the twenty-dollar bill. He is a loving God-one Whose desire is to see integrity grow in our minds and hearts. Choosing to do the right thing, especially in questionable circumstances, is what determines a person's honorability. Don't you agree?

- Have you ever had an experience like my Dad had with stealing?

- If so, how did you handle the dishonor?

- Do you feel you made the right decision?

- How would that scenario look if you had changed the outcome to a positive one?

- If you can honestly say you have never stolen anything, have you harshly judged others for their lack of judgment when you learned of their misbehavior?

HONOR

WORD SEARCH

```
C E B V Y T R W Q A H A
D I G N I T Y R S J C S
E L O R R T H A N K O T
T U F F P B E R N A M N
N D B A R L Y O R L P A
A M N U O L W K D E L V
S E A W T L Q C X L I R
M E S A E P U R E G M E
D T C D C E U Y Q Z E S
A S G N T C M E R P N B
F E B H J C R E D I T O
R E O B E D I E N T N D
F A J U M H Z M G T P L
```

DIGNITY	PROTECT	OBSERVANT
ACKNOWLEDGE	ESTEEM	COMPLIMENT
THANK	OBEDIENT	CREDIT

DAY 4

Honor Family

But how should you honor your brother or sister? The Bible tells us, "Finally, all of you, have unity of mind, sympathy, brotherly love, a tender heart, and a humble mind. Do not repay evil for evil or reviling for reviling, but on the contrary, bless, for to this you were called, that you may obtain a blessing" (*1 Peter 3:8-9* ESV).

Dad recalled a time in his youth when he was put in charge of his brothers. While their parents were away, an uprising occurred. The brothers pushed him out of the house and locked the door behind him. Later, hearing different sides of the story, I concluded that Dad might have been too bossy.

Can you see this in your relationship with your siblings or friends? Nobody wants to be controlled. It doesn't work. I mean, siblings are not robots that you control remotely (though sometimes we'd like that, right?). We were created individually, which means there are no two exactly alike, including twins. This means that we may think similarly on some levels, but at other times we may think quite the opposite.

Would you say then that mutual respect and honoring the other person's ideas just *might* be the key to healthy relationships? The same is true of your relationships with others. You want to create a positive flow of respect among those you communicate with.

Opposites

Draw a line between the left-hand and right-hand columns connecting the honor word with its opposite. Use a thesaurus if you'd like.

LISTEN

COMPLIMENT

FAIR

LOYAL

INTEGRITY

UPRIGHT

ADMIRABLE

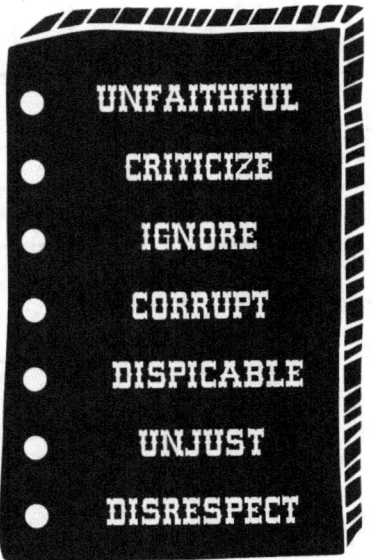

UNFAITHFUL

CRITICIZE

IGNORE

CORRUPT

DISPICABLE

UNJUST

DISRESPECT

HONOR MAZE

Help KIM reach the key to wisdom.
Keep track of how many keys KIM has collected on page 125....

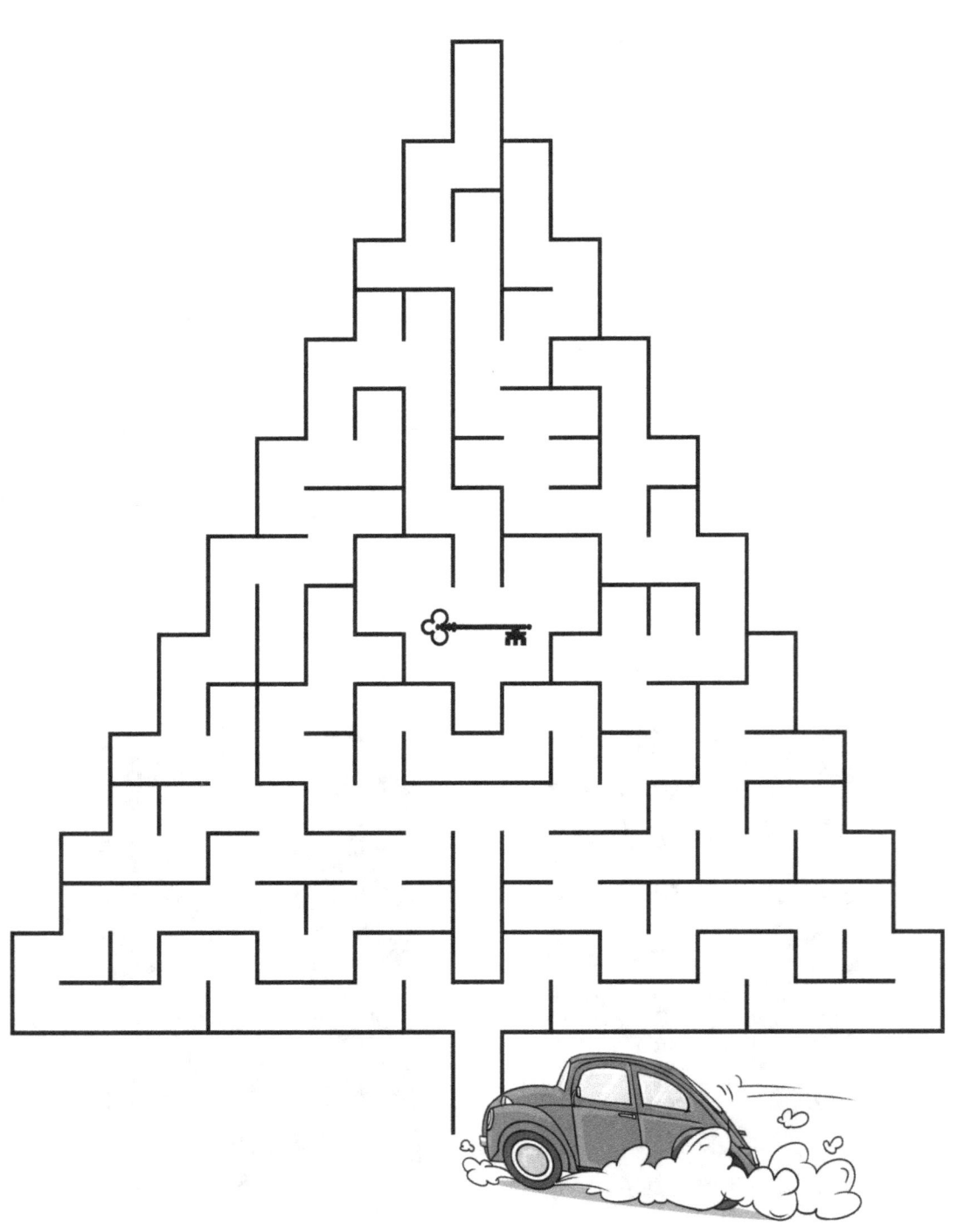

DAY 5

Listen Attentively

Have you ever been lying on a blanket out underneath the stars? Do you remember becoming aware of the sounds around you more vividly than is common? Pretty cool, wasn't it? Maybe you heard a TV or people talking in the distance, a car horn, or a dog barking. The point is that you heard sounds you may typically have dismissed. When you listen attentively, you understand much better what others are trying to communicate.

My dad taught us good listening skills when we went hiking. I didn't pay attention to my steps and how loud I was crunching through the dead branches and leaves. While I listened to Dad's instructions, it began to sink into my thinking that I needed to be a better listener. And not just for hiking. Did I listen to my friends and parents in general? Or was I more self-absorbed? It was certain that I'd have plenty of time to ponder the lesson that weekend.

Listening attentively to those around us is much the same way as us kids taking direction from my dad. If we are tromping over the words of others, all we can hear is our own noise. We each need to be thoughtful before those words come out of our mouths. What we have to say is important, but sometimes we can honor another by just listening.

Check the True or False box for each statement.

T   F

Kindess is weakness.

You should always have the first say in a conversation.

Honor is a strength.

Doing the right thing is a good thing.

Conversations are best when you're angry.

Ignoring the needs of others is helpful.

Listening builds better relationships.

HONOR
Code Breaker

Use the key below to break the code.

A	B	C	D	E	F	G	H	I	J	K	L	M
N	O	P	Q	R	S	T	U	V	W	X	Y	Z

"

"

DAY 6

Keep Commitments

"If a man vows a vow to the Lord, or swears an oath to bind himself by a pledge, he shall not break his word. He shall do according to all that proceeds out of his mouth" (*Numbers 30:2 ESV*). This doesn't just apply to men. Keeping commitments shows respect. Dad taught us, kids, to show up early to an event—never late. If we were unable to meet our commitment, we'd be expected to let the other party know with as much notice as possible to create only a minor inconvenience. This is what common courtesy is all about. Is it like this in your family as well? I admit this is one I still struggle with. I try to fit too many events into a given time slot and sometimes find myself arriving late.

REFLECTION TIME

Let's 'put the shoe on the other foot' for a minute while we consider how it makes you feel when the other party dismisses their commitment to you.

Have you ever been 'blown off' by a friend who neglected to tell you she didn't want to hang out after all? What reaction describes your feelings best?
Angry?____ Frustrated?____ Sad?____ Fearful?____ Don't care?____

You are at the movies waiting for a friend to meet you there. Out of kindness, you buy their ticket too, expecting them any time now. The friend never texts or calls to let you know they aren't coming. What reaction describes your feelings best?
Anger?____ Frustrated?____ Sad?____ Fearful?____ Don't care?____

You and your friends have decided to have a bake sale to earn money for a school trip. You all agreed to show up early to get everything set up. On the day of the sale, they show up an hour late for no 'legit' reason. What reaction describes your feelings best?
Anger?____ Frustrated?____ Sad?____ Fearful?____ Don't care?____

Can you think of a time when you haven't kept your commitment? Yes or No _____
If yes, how do you think that made the other person feel? _____

Keeping your word is important, isn't it? The more you follow through on your commitments, the more you build healthy relationships with others who believe they can count on you. You are showing yourself to be dependable.

Check the boxes that are true for you.

I can...	I can do this very well	I can do this fairly well	I can do this with some help	I need more practice
Honor God				
Obey my parents				
Be Trustworthy				
Honor Family				
Listen Attentively				
Keep Commitments				

Complete the table below.

I can be honorable by	
One thing I need to improve	
To improve I can	
At least one person I need to honor	

DAY 7

Honor Family Heritage and Traditions

One thing we all have in common is family. And with family comes history and tradition. You may have come from a big family with lots of cousins. Or perhaps you are an only child with older parents and never got to know your grandparents. Your family might be somewhere in-between these scenarios. But there's one thing I know: God loves variety. We need not look any further than our immediate family to notice all the differences among our loved ones. If we zoom out far enough, we see the variation our loving Creator has brought about: We see wonderful diversity all around, and not only with people . . . It's with *everything*!

God's desire to have a family goes w-a-a-a-y back. Just look at this passage written by David in the book of Psalms: "For you created my inmost being; you knit me together in my mother's womb. Your eyes saw my unformed body; all the days ordained for me were written in your book before one of them came to be" (*Psalm 139: 13, 16* NIV).

Does knowing that we were ALL made by the same God who desired to have a family give you pause to think about the division in races? He purposefully and thoughtfully made each of our skin tones unique and beautiful, as he desired.

Each family brings unique characteristics and strengths to the 'world's table.' We each have traditions that we hold dear. It's important to recognize and honor each other for these differences. We have so much to learn from each other. Your call to action is this: Your generation must continue strengthening the bonds of unity with your brothers and sisters of all ethnic groups. It is quite possible to maintain our family traditions and cultures while still honoring other families for theirs.

Name a family tradition you enjoy. _____

Name a family tradition you would like to start in your family. _____

Think about a schoolmate from a different religion than yours. What question would you like to ask them if you had the opportunity? _____

If you could travel to another country to experience a different culture, where would it be and why? _____

_____

Take some time to talk to your parents or grandparents about their experiences growing up. I'm sure you will find some of their stories very interesting. Honor them by showing your interest and good questions. You'll be amazed. I'm certain of that!

HONOR KEY

How honorable are you? Circle the best answer for each scenario.

1. Your mom asks you to clean your room before supper. Do you...

Ignore her.	Watch TV longer, then clean your room.	Obey right away.	Tell her, "No, thank you."
A	B	C	D

2. You see money fall out of somebody's pocket. Do you...

Take it for your own.	Kindly hand it back to them letting them know they dropped it.	Wait to see if anyone picks it up.	Give it back to them only if it's coins.
A	B	C	D

3. When you come to a doorway at the same time as a girl and boy. Do you...

Push your way through first.	Open the door for the girl but not the boy.	Keep talking on your phone and ignore them completely.	Let both pass through the door before you do.
A	B	C	D

4. Your schoolmate is getting bullied. Do you...

Bring it to the attention of the teacher.	It's not your problem. Don't worry about it.	Do nothing for fear you'll get bullied too.	Kick the bully in the shin and run.
A	B	C	D

5. At the dinner table with family, you want a breadstick that's out of reach. Do you...

Stand and stretch over the table to get it.	Ask the person nearest to throw it to you.	Ask the person nearest, "Please, pass the breadsticks."	Walk around the table and get it yourself.
A	B	C	D

6. You told your dad you'd take out the trash. Do you...

Take out the trash.	Make excuses.	Wait till he reminds you.	Keep watching TV and forget about it.
A	B	C	D

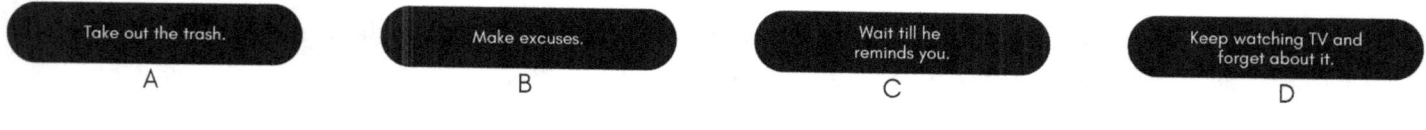

Talk about your answers with a parent, grandparent, or mentor.

HONOR
QUIZ KEY

On the Honor quiz page, you circled A, B, C or D for each scenario.

You can see below that each letter is = to a number from 0 to 3

In the 'Points' box, write the number = to the letter
you circled for each scenario in the quiz.

Next, add the numbers together at the bottom for your total.

1. A=0 B=2 C=3 D=1

2. A=0 B=3 C=2 D=1

3. A=0 B=2 C=1 D=3

4. A=3 B=0 C=2 D=1

5. A=2 B=1 C=3 D=0

6. A=3 B=1 C=2 D=0

Points

+ _____

Next, write your total from this page in the Honor
box on page 123 to calculate your overall score.

Total

Spring branding, Separ, New Mexico, 1963

May family brand

HOSPITALITY

Left to right: Dad, Grandpa R.B., and Uncle David round up the cattle.

HOSPITALITY

A Cowboy Story

The monsoon rains had yet to bless the dry land. Spring was in the rear-view mirror now as the days grew longer. The crystal blue sky would soon display its vibrant hue as the day's first light rose on the horizon. Cold morning temperatures insisted you stay under the bed-covers till it warmed up a little. But the ranchers were already saddling up their horses for the day's work. Spring had witnessed the birth of dozens of Hereford calves, all of which needed vaccinations, tagging, and branding.

Once they arrived, the men built a campfire in the corral at East Camp. With a few spoons of coffee, a half jug of water, and some red, glowing coals, the old tin pot brewed a 'mean' cup of coffee that took the chill off the morning—and warmed the bellies of the men.

They swapped a few jokes and tall tales while sipping the steamy beverage. Undoubtedly, it would be a long, dusty day of hard work. Grandpa, Dad, his two brothers, and ranchers invited from nearby shared something other than camaraderie and kinship. Visions began to stir in their minds as they looked forward to the noon meal we would cater for them. Undoubtedly, it would be the highlight of their day.

Grandpa grew up in this southwestern New Mexico desert in the 1920s. He could tell you where every fence corner or windmill was located. He was a skilled cattleman and horse whisperer—long before most folks knew what a horse whisperer was. He was well-known in the area, and his neighbors knew they could count on him in their time of need.

Grandpa wasn't notably talkative—But when he spoke, folks listened. Naturally, he taught his three boys the ranching life while exemplifying integrity, respect, and hospitable ways. Dad used to tell the story that if he slept in, Grandpa would come into his bedroom, gently grab his big toe, wiggle it, and say, "You gonna come to work with me today?" Of course, Dad got right up. All three siblings wanted to make their dad proud.

Back at the house, Grandma and Mom were 'cooking up a storm.' As a six-year-old, I, too, was given helper duties. The flavor-filled aromas that wafted through the house made my mouth water so badly. I could almost taste the German Chocolate cake coming out of the oven.

We worked throughout the morning as we prepared the feast to feed the working cattlemen. A big pot of pinto beans—sorted and soaked the night before—simmered on the stove. On the back burner were tea bags steeping to make a gallon of sweet tea. The perfectly formed and baked homemade yeast rolls were pulled from the oven and replaced by a green chili enchilada casserole waiting its turn to bake. Additionally, we sliced onions and tomatoes to add to the meal. The two-layered cake was baked early that morning, giving it ample cooling time before the middle and outside layers were frosted.

We loaded up the meal and all the fixings in Grandpa's old powder-blue step-side Chevy pickup truck: Destination, East Camp. I sat with the gallon of tea steadied between my feet on the floorboard. Mom held the cake in her lap. The rest of the meal was tin-foiled and boxed up in the truck bed.

Grandma hopped in the driver's seat. The truck *puttered* along the well-rutted dirt road with which that vehicle was so familiar. We drove slowly enough to avoid creating a thick cloud of dust around the food, but they could see us coming from a mile away. We were a welcome sight to those hungry cowboys!

On arrival, we pulled the truck tailgate down and spread a tablecloth over it to provide a makeshift serving table for all the food we had prepared. Meanwhile, the men took their hats off and washed up to prepare for the meal. The neighboring ranchers always looked forward with great anticipation to the meals Grandma made. She always ensured they were well-fed and satisfied. With their bellies full, they would finish out their workday strong.

For six-year-old me, the cows at the Camp were big and scary. "Momma, they're lookin' at me," I remember saying—because I was so afraid. I stayed close to the adults in the event one cow decided to come closer for a visit. The 'fellers' loved the home-cooked meal, thanking us heartily as they helped clean up afterward. Looking back over the pickup seat as we girls drove away, I saw the cowboys put their hats back on as they turned to go back to work.

DAY 1

Prepare Your Heart

Hospitality is more than just inviting your friend for a sleepover. In advance of the friend and before the invitation, there is one thing you need to do: *Prepare your heart.* I bet you are thinking, "It's just a sleepover. What does that have to do with my heart?"

Hospitality creates a comfortable atmosphere regardless of where you are—or who is with you. But your heart has to be in it. Let's say you have a dog. He rolled in something that smelled stinky and needed a bath. Do you ignore the smell and expect someone else in your family to wash him? Or perhaps you take him outside to the garden hose, drizzle water over him, and call it 'done.' Or maybe you have the water, but don't think about that soap, brush, and towels that are also needed. You see, your heart condition determines how prepared you are. If your heart's in the right place, you will have all the necessary items to care for your dog properly.

The same rule applies to family. When your mom or dad are making supper, could they use your help? And what about helping wash the dishes afterward? Sitting in front of the television is easier, but is that the right thing to do? And what if you notice your sibling's arms are overloaded? Would you ignore it, or would you help by lightening their load? Could your 'heart attitude' use a change?

Upon your friend's arrival, giving them a warm welcome is only the beginning of your sleepover. Have you considered what will bring joy to your guest? Could you help your parents prepare your friend's favorite meal? Name some ways you can improve your heart attitude

----

Color the picture below. As you do, be mindful while considering some ways you can be hospitable.

DAY 2

Prepare A Place

The Scripture, *Luke 6:38* ESV, explains what giving and receiving is like: "Give and it will be given to you. Good measure, pressed down, shaken together, running over, will be put into your lap. For with the measure you use it will be measured back to you." It doesn't say that things will be put in your lap when you stand back and let others do for you. Not at all. It says that you will get back what you give-in equal measure.

The goal is not to be hospitable to your guests in hopes that they'll treat you the same way when you go to their homes. The real purpose is giving your time and energy to make sure your guest feels love. This principle is exemplified in the parable about the good Samaritan (*Luke 10: 27-37*), who takes care of a traveler who was beaten up on the roadside. He cares for the traveler's wounds, carries him to town, and pays the innkeeper to look after him. In this story, the good Samaritan 'goes above and beyond' to show the traveler his love.

Now, let's consider your guests. Here are some quick questions to ask yourself:
- Have you made sure the bedding is clean?
- What about your room? Have you arranged it to sufficiently accomodate a guest?
- Did you have chores to complete before the friend's arrival?
- Will you help your parents prepare a meal or two to feed them?
- What about food sensitivities or religious food exceptions?
- What will you do when you're together? Will your friend enjoy these activities?

Turn This Scene Around

Several friends are at your home for a sleepover. One friend trash-talks your sister. You feel uncomfortable but don't say anything. Then your friend suggests playing a mean prank on her. Your friend has gone too far. You 'blow up' in anger and yell at her.

Now, when I snap my finger, your attitude changes from one of anger to forgiveness and kindness. How does your attitude look now? Explain below. Ready...and...

_____

_____

_____

HOSPITALITY SCRAMBLE

Unscramble the words in the first row by connecting them with their match on the right.

PICSOOMANS	GREETING
DANGIDNUSERTN	ATTENTION
NITAETONT	COMPASSION
YESCUROT	UNDERSTANDING
SOWHEFLIPL	CONSIDERATE
TEGGRINE	FELLOWSHIP
TEADERSINCO	COURTESY

DAY 3

Encourage Conversation

Conversation involves word choice, listening, and speaking. It is also influenced by your body language, tone of voice, and facial expression. Shrugging your shoulders is a response, as is rolling your eyes and walking away from the person you were chatting with. But is this the type of conversation that brings about friendly relationships?

In "A Cowboy Story," I described how the neighbor ranchers looked forward to helping. It was not only the neighborly thing to offer help, but the men also enjoyed the day's fellowship. While they enjoyed a delicious home-cooked meal, the cowboys' conversation topics included family, the work at hand, and our country's state of affairs. They even exchanged jokes. All the neighbors felt welcome and appreciated. Hospitality manifested itself in cordial communication and mutual respect.

What do the conversations sound like in your world? The boxes ☑ next to the characteristics that apply to your personality. This exercise is to increase awareness of your conversational skills.

☐ Reserved	☐ Laid-back	☐ Mean
☐ Unpleasant	☐ Insensitive	☐ Soft-spoken
☐ Bitter	☐ Light-hearted	☐ Inspiring
☐ Encouraging	☐ Passive	☐ Discouraging
☐ Kind	☐ Amusing	☐ Friendly
☐ Loud	☐ Caring	☐ Uninterested

Be thoughtful about the following questions. Consider how you can use the power of your words to build healthy communication with others.

- How would you begin a respectful, convincing conversation with an adult about your favorite kind of music?

  _____

- Give an example of how you would inspire a friend today.

  _____

- Write three kind things you could say to an older adult to brighten their day.

  _____

- What words would you use to welcome your guest to your home?

  _____

HOSPITALITY

WORD SEARCH

```
W  R  G  L  A  I  D  R  O  C  A  B
A  L  M  T  R  N  G  T  H  R  C  V
V  P  R  E  P  A  R  E  Y  N  M  Y
K  G  R  E  E  T  A  X  Q  Y  Z  T
U  R  N  M  L  Y  C  Z  L  L  Q  I
R  O  X  C  V  B  I  R  P  D  B  L
W  A  T  H  C  M  O  E  M  N  P  A
Y  L  X  L  X  B  U  W  E  E  H  T
E  O  N  P  H  W  S  V  Y  I  G  I
N  F  A  G  P  U  Q  A  P  R  Q  P
B  F  I  W  F  Z  O  R  O  F  Z  S
A  E  Q  V  I  N  V  I  T  E  P  O
N  R  P  L  U  M  K  N  M  G  K  H
```

HOSPITALITY	NEIGHBORLY	CORDIAL
FRIENDLY	OFFER	PREPARE
INVITE	GREET	GRACIOUS

DAY 4

Share What You Have

Let's talk for a minute about sharing. We are taught when we're young to share our toys and play nicely with our siblings and friends. But are toys all we are supposed to share?

This Bible scripture nails it. "Each one of you should give what you have decided in your heart to give. You should not give if it makes you unhappy or if you feel forced to give. God loves those who are happy to give" (*2 Corinthians 9:7* NLT).

Using this Scripture as our guide, let's broaden our imagination and think of ways we can willingly share what we have with others. List the tangibles (things you can touch, like toys) and intangibles (stuff you *can't* touch, like ideas). Make your answers personal with your individual abilities.

Tangibles_____

_____

Intangibles_____

_____

Opposites

Draw a line between the left-hand and right-hand columns connecting the hospitality word with its opposite. Use a thesaurus if you'd like.

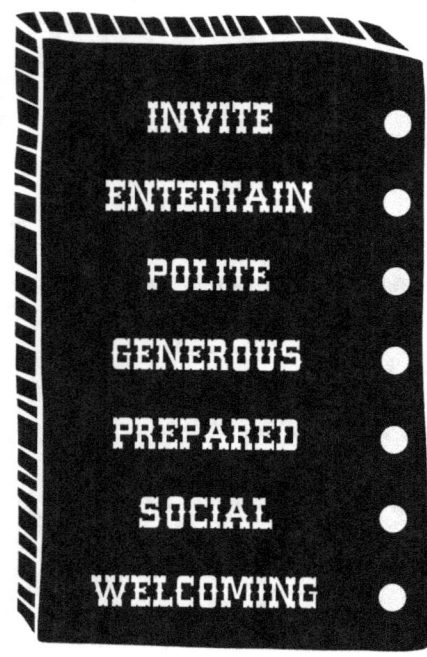

INVITE

ENTERTAIN

POLITE

GENEROUS

PREPARED

SOCIAL

WELCOMING

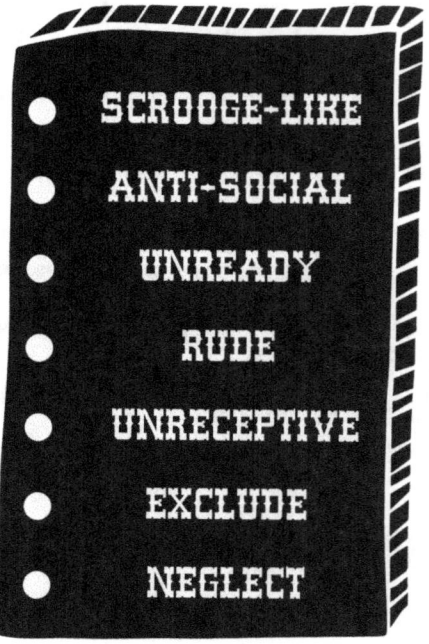

SCROOGE-LIKE

ANTI-SOCIAL

UNREADY

RUDE

UNRECEPTIVE

EXCLUDE

NEGLECT

HOSPITALITY MAZE

Help KIM reach the key to wisdom.
Keep track of how many keys KIM has collected on page 125....

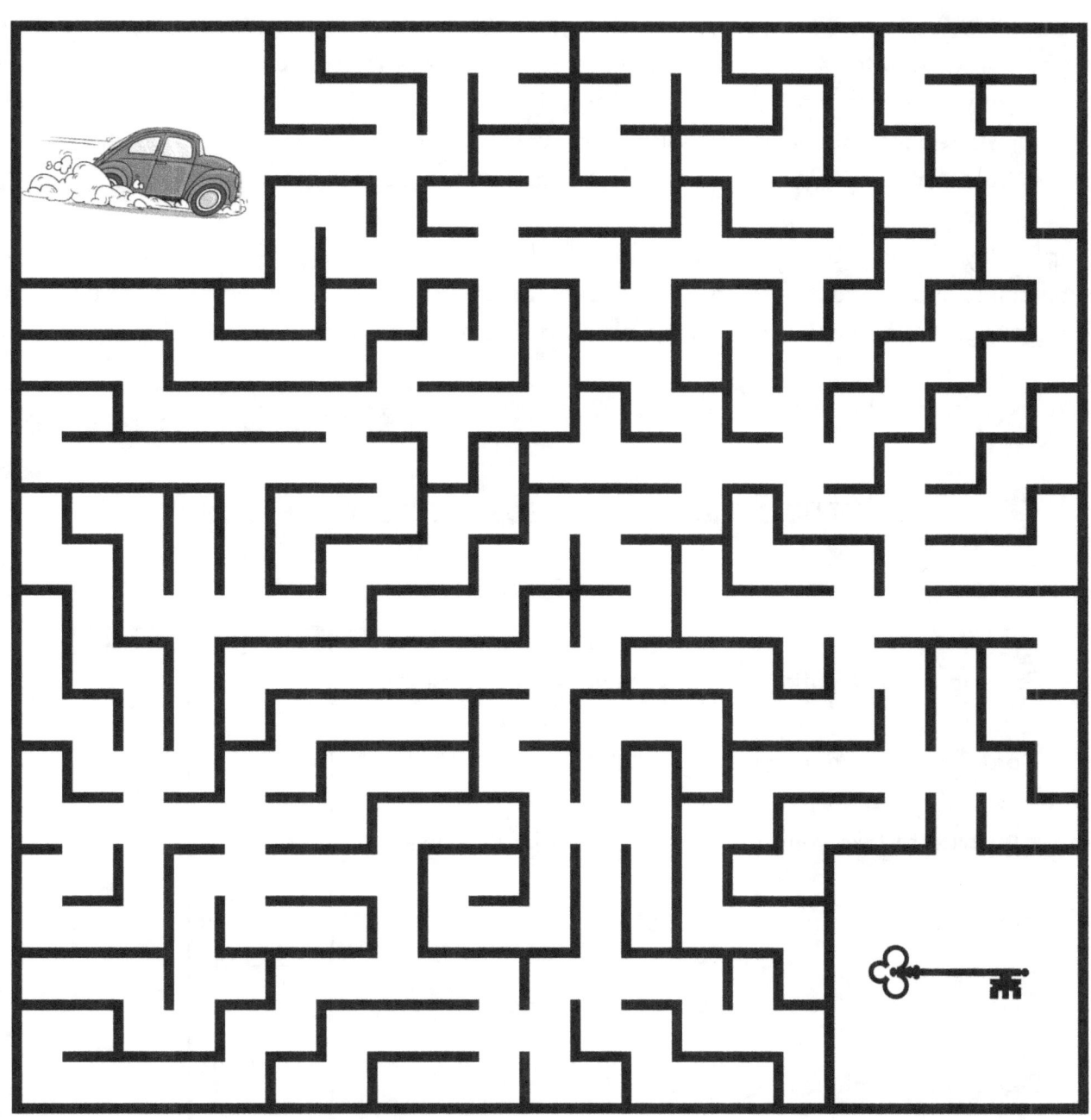

DAY 5

Be Willing To Adapt

When faced with a new challenge, do you dig your heels in and refuse to change even though you know it would be a better outcome? Maybe you don't have a direction, but you're okay with whatever the challenge brings. The bottom line with hospitality is that you must be willing to adapt.

It's Saturday. You've invited your friend, Jimmy, over to watch a movie. When Jimmy shows up, he asks if you want to toss the football in the backyard instead. You're not feeling it. You were looking forward to the movie, but this is where the art of hospitality comes in. This is when you put Jimmy's request above your desire. You want him to enjoy his time at your house. Tell Jimmy, "Sure. Let's do it. Then after a while, we can watch the movie."

Adaptability doesn't mean you have to change who you are. Family traditions, religious ceremonies, and your extraordinary personality remain the same. Adapting means you want to make your guests feel at ease like you would want to be treated if you were in their home.

On a scale from 1 - 10, what is your adaptability level? ❶ ❷ ❸ ❹ ❺ ❻ ❼ ❽ ❾ ❿

Check the True or False box for each statement.

	T	F
Starting a conversation can make your guest at ease.	☐	☐
Cordial means warm and sincere.	☐	☐
It is polite to take your friend's earbuds without asking.	☐	☐
When you serve others, it is a kindness.	☐	☐
Treat your guest like you'd want to be treated.	☐	☐
Being rude to others is highly advised.	☐	☐
Ignoring your friend builds a better relationship.	☐	☐

Use the key below to break the code.

A	B	C	D	E	F	G	H	I	J	K	L	M
N	O	P	Q	R	S	T	U	V	W	X	Y	Z

  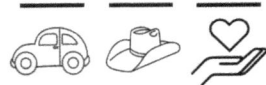

AND DO NOT

NEGLECT DOING

GOOD AND SHARING

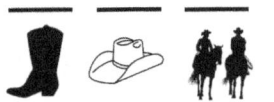  

FOR WITH SUCH

SACRIFICES GOD

IS PLEASED.

DAY 6

Serve Willingly

One of my favorite Scripture passages is: " For you were called to freedom, brothers. Only do not let your freedom *become* an opportunity for the flesh, but through love serve one another." (*Galatians 5:13* LEB).

Growing up in the USA in the '60s and '70s, life was pretty free. Skating, biking, and riding horses were our outlets. And for the most part, I bet you, too, have spare time to do what you want. I imagine you have chores or weekly duties to help the family—but have you ever considered outside that box of responsibilities? How about serving friends, family, and your community in some helpful way?

Consider ways you could use your freedom for the good of others In the next paragraph, you will read a few good ideas. You can use your imagination and see what you come up with.

- Grab a trash bag and head out to the roadside. Litter is a big problem. But even fifteen minutes per weekend around your neighborhood would help to make your area look more respectable.
- Volunteer at your local nursing home. Call and ask how you could help. If you cannot physically go there, try writing a card or drawing a picture and mailing it to the home. The patients who live there love to get mail.
- Do you live near your grandparents? How about offering to pick up loose tree limbs or rake fallen leaves to remove them from their yard?
- Do you have a younger sibling? Read to them. Spend time teaching them something you know.

 **REFLECTION TIME**

How does it make you feel when you witness someone throw trash out their car window? Angry? ____ Sad? ____ Don't care? ____ Frustrated? ____ Agree? ____
Can you pick up the trash they left behind? Yes ____ No ____

Your dad instructs you to help your mom in the kitchen. What is your reaction?
Anger?____ Sad? ____ Don't care? ____ Frustrated? ____ Agreeable? ____
Could helping-even at home-be an act of service? Yes ____ or No ____

Your uncle served in the war and wants to share the story of his service to our country. Are you disinterested? ____ A willing and good listener? ____ Don't care? ____
Could hearing your uncle's stories make your relationship stronger? Could it help you gain some experience with the way other people find their place in serving? We can certainly learn a lot from those who have served our country before us.

HOSPITALITY
Self Evaluation Worksheet

Check the boxes that are true for you.

I can...	I can do this very well	I can do this fairly well	I can do this with some help	I need more practice
Prepare my heart				
Prepare a place				
Encourage conversation				
Share what I have				
Be willing to adapt				
Serve willingly				

Complete the table below.

I can be helpful by doing or saying	
One thing I need to improve	
To improve I can	
One way to encourage another	

DAY 7

Invite Others Into Your Family

What does your family do that is unique? Are you sports people? Book readers? Craft makers? TV watchers? Game players? Garden tenders? Campers? Musicians? Whatever your family background, I know you have something unique to your family that you could share with others.

You might remember in the book's introduction that we made a tradition of doing the 'Hokey Pokey' before starting our family reunion prayer time. Wouldn't you agree that this is super-unique? The thing is, we do the 'Hokey Pokey' when we have close friends over as well. This open invitation to our friends makes them a part of our family for the day. As you can imagine, it brings a smile to every face—and laughter 'to boot!'

Consider your family's uniqueness. List at least three things you enjoy doing as a family that you could share with a guest and help them to feel welcome. _____
_____

Do you feel awkward when your guests come over to visit? I can assure you that you're not alone. The best way to overcome this feeling is to be yourself and focus on making your guest feel like family. List at least three ways you can make this happen. _____
_____

We enjoy board games in our family. Games amuse and entertain a wide range of people. Which game is your family's favorite? _____ Games are also good ice-breakers. They help you and your guests to relax.

The kitchen can be a fun place to entertain. With your parent's or guardian's supervision, there are countless recipes to try. Pizzas and cookies are fun to bake. Smoothies are easy to make. The point is that every family eats something. What would you make?
_____

There are plenty of ways to entertain your guests outside: Hiking, biking, and swimming, are just a few. If you could choose any outdoor activity, which would be your favorite? _____ Would your choice be the same for your guest? ____ If not, what would you choose? _____

HSPITALITY KEY

How hospitable are you? Circle the best answer for each scenario.

1. Your grandparents come for a visit to your home. Do you...

Greet them at the door and welcome them inside.	Disregard them and keep playing on your phone.	Hide out in your bedroom.	Open the door for them, then walk away without inviting them inside.
A	B	C	D

2. Your best friend comes over for supper. Do you...

Make him wait till you've finished eating to fill his plate.	Figure it's every man for himself.	Fill your plate before your friend.	Invite him to fill his plate before yours.
A	B	C	D

3. There are six chairs and seven friends. Do you...

Grab one fast like the game, Musical Chairs.	Pull the chair out from under someone so you can sit down.	Offer to stand so your friends can sit.	Ignore the issue all together.
A	B	C	D

4. You have a friend over for the night. Do you...

Let them fend for themselves.	Offer them your bed-You lay out a bedroll on the floor for you.	Give them your bed but take the bed covers for you on the floor.	Wait for Mom to resolve the issue.
A	B	C	D

5. It's time to feed the pets. Do you...

Ignore them-after all, they ate yesterday.	Make sure they have the proper amount of food and water.	Carelessly slop food around the bowl and slosh the water.	Say, "It's not my turn to feed. You do it."
A	B	C	D

6. It's the last piece of pizza. Do you...

Do nothing because you have had your fill.	Lick it so no one else will want it but you.	Eat it quick before anyone notices.	Offer the last piece to everyone else first.
A	B	C	D

Talk about your answers with a parent, grandparent, or mentor.

HOSPITALITY
QUIZ KEY

On the Hospitality quiz page, you circled A, B, C or D for each scenario.

You can see below that each letter is = to a number from 0 to 3

In the 'Points' box, write the number = to the letter
you circled for each scenario in the quiz.

Next, add the numbers together at the bottom for your total.

1. A=3 B=0 C=1 D=2

2. A=0 B=1 C=2 D=3

3. A=2 B=0 C=3 D=1

4. A=0 B=3 C=1 D=2

5. A=0 B=3 C=2 D=1

6. A=2 B=0 C=1 D=3

Points

+ _____

Total

Next, write your total from this page in the
Hospitality box on page 123 to
calculate your overall score.

Dad's spot landing in his Cessna 182

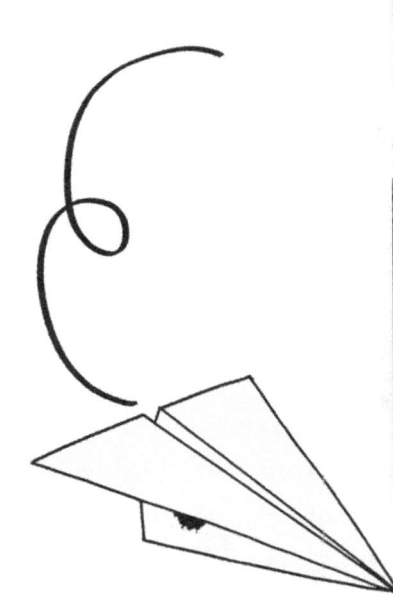

Pilot's license

DEMING (N.M.) GRAPHIC, OCTOBER 21, 1968

Buris May received his private pilot's license Thursday following completion of the Deming Flying Service pilot's school. Jack Morrow, a student in the school, soloed Sept. 23.

Dad's pilot's license

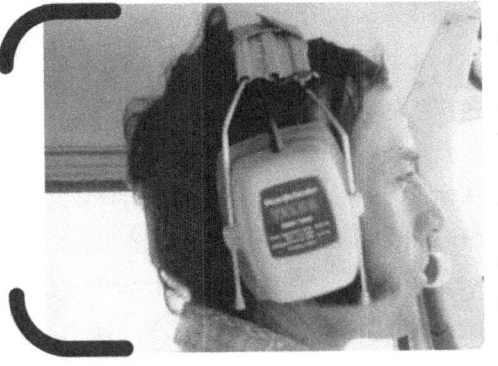

Dad in the pilot seat

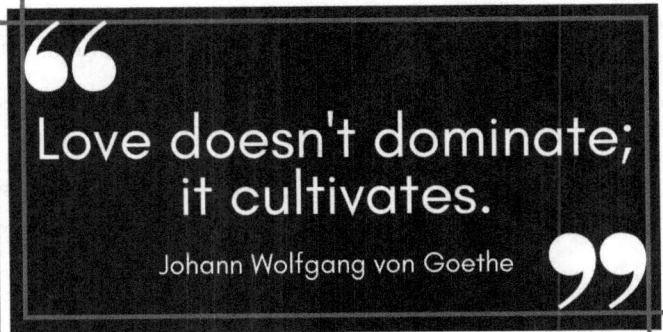

> **Love doesn't dominate; it cultivates.**
>
> Johann Wolfgang von Goethe

CULTIVATION

Flying With Dad

There was an advertisement for 'A-Penny-a-Pound Ride' for an airplane flight. It was 1965, and the tri-county fair was in town. That day, Dad and Mom's adventurous flight through the clear blue New Mexico sky was short but thrilling—giving them ear-to-ear grins. Following that memorable flight, Mom reported that Dad had been so excited that he'd jumped up and down with delight, proclaiming he would become a pilot. That flight stirred a desire in Dad that led to the purchase of his first co-owned airplane, a Piper Tri-pacer. Our family scrapbook holds the newspaper clipping that showed the pilot's license Dad earned three years later, on October 17, 1968.

I was in my momma's womb the first time I was air bound. Naturally, my love of flying goes way back. Our family took many flights together in Dad's Cessna 182, a small aircraft he bought in my youth, which carried our family of five quite snuggly. My older brother usually called middle as he figured he had seniority in his claims. My sister and I were in the window seats—jam-packed like a package of Easter Peeps with little wiggle room.

If you've ever been in an airplane, especially the smaller ones, you know turbulence can be problematic. Sometimes, the air pockets were so bad that we wondered if the seat belts would be enough to keep our heads from going through the roof. Another side effect of turbulence for us was air sickness. We always stocked gallon Ziploc bags lined with a diaper to catch the unfortunate air passengers 'tossed cookies.' Of course, with vomiting occurring in such a small space, I'm sure you can imagine how a 'gagging party' would probably follow. We got used to throwing up being an unfortunate event that occurred sometimes.

My most exciting times flying happened when Dad would fly me to my orthodontic appointments. Does that sound strange to you? I don't doubt it. Looking back, I realize how rare and precious those moments were. Our family had moved a long, four-hour drive away from my orthodontist. However, my folks had already paid for my braces.

So they continued my visits to the same doctor for the rest of my time in braces. Every couple of months, Dad and I would take the day off from work and school, hop on his motorcycle, and drive to the airport. Then, off we'd fly, destination-bound. We had extended family on the other side that would pick us up after our thirty-seven-minute flight and then transport us to my appointments.

Flying beside Dad as a co-pilot was a blast! We navigated the skies as he taught me basic skills using his calming demeanor and guidance. He was a patient and loving instructor. Still, there was so much to learn. Flying at our desired altitude one day, Dad lightheartedly said, "Let me show you a little something." He pivoted the ignition key one turn to the left. Shortly, the propeller came to a complete stop. My heart must have skipped a beat. It quickly dawned on me that we weren't falling out of the sky as you'd expect. Wide-eyed, I looked at Dad's grinning face with amazement. He explained that the plane would glide until it lost altitude with decreased speed. A short time later, he turned the key over once again. To my relief, the propeller fired right up.

Dad had one more trick up his sleeve during that trip. He showed me how to stall the engine. He pulled back on the yoke as we climbed in elevation with the plane's nose upward. At that steep ascension, the plane naturally stalled out. Once again, the propeller stopped spinning. At this moment, my stomach flipped. As he brought the nose downward, bringing us back to the desired altitude, he turned the engine on again—And off we flew!

Dad would often let me fly the plane. Occasionally, he would get into a relaxed position, putting a small pillow under his head. He would point off in the distance, "Head to the left side of that mountain." Then, he'd close his eyes and take a nap, leaving me in charge of piloting the aircraft. Now, whether or not he actually fell asleep is anybody's guess. I suspect he kept one eye open. But these flights with Dad began to cultivate a sense of confidence in me that I continued to build upon as I grew up. *Yeah.* My dad was cool like that!

DAY 1

Stand For What Is Right

Cultural norms today may seem morally corrupt compared to past generations. But the truth is, we have always seen right and wrong, truth and lies, virtuous and disreputable people. It is our choice to determine which camp we'll join.

To use the metaphor of a compass in this lesson, North stands for what is right, South stands for what is wrong, and East and West stand for sitting on the fence and being indifferent. The slippery slope comes when we divert our thinking into believing that East, West, or South are good directions. People said to have no moral compass often make bad choices. When your compass needle begins to change from a spot-on northward direction to one of poor judgment, that's the time to stop, think about the consequences, then choose to stand for what is right.

The same goes for choosing your friends carefully. *1 Corinthians 15:33* NIV advises, "Do not be misled: 'Bad company corrupts good character.'" Standing for what's right is not always the easiest route to navigate—But it's always the wisest."

Have you ever had to make a tough choice that went against a popular decision because you knew it wasn't right? If so, you get a star for bravery. Seriously . . . Kudos to you! It is challenging, especially for your age, to stand out when you'd rather just fit in. Jesus described it well in *Matthew 7:13-14* LEB, "Enter through the narrow gate, because broad is the gate and spacious is the road that leads to destruction, and there are many who enter through it, because narrow is the gate and constricted is the road that leads to life, and there are few who find it!" Orient your compass needle to stand for what is right. Soon, it will become a way of life. As an added bonus, you will positively influence your friends.

Color the picture below. As you do, be mindful as you consider ways to cultivate good relationships.

DAY 2

Choose Peace Over Conflict

Have you ever flown in an airplane? If so, what was your experience?
Scary___? Calm___? Turbulent___? Easy going___?
What do you imagine it would be like if you haven't flown before?

_____

I have experienced peace, fear, awe, thrill, and turbulence when flying. On the peaceful flights, Dad allowed us to take off our seatbelts. But when turmoil would arise from the clouds or rain, we would have to fasten our seatbelts for safety. That's because when flying in a smaller plane that hits turbulence, you could almost hit your head on the frame of the plane if you're not buckled in.

Peace is a choice, isn't it? This doesn't mean just 'going with the flow' to avoid conflict. Inner peace is a deliberate mindset that allows you to be self-controlled even when the situations you face are problematic.

Think of a time when you disagreed with a friend or family member. Did the conflict intensify as you tried to get your point across? Now, think of a conversation with that same person where there was no conflict. Words were exchanged with kindness and respect, right? Cultivating peace in your life is so much easier—and certainly more gratifying—than cultivating conflict. *2 Corinthians 13:11* MSG counsels us, "And that's about it, friends. Be cheerful. Keep things in good repair. Keep your spirits up. Think in harmony. Be agreeable. Do all that, and the God of love and peace will be with you for sure."

Turn This Scene Around

Your little brother accuses you of taking the TV remote. You claim you don't have it. His voice gets louder, "I saw you with it earlier!" You yell back at him, "I DON'T HAVE THE REMOTE," leaving the room angry and frustrated. Now, when I snap my finger, your attitude changes from anger to a peaceful solution. How do you handle yourself now? Explain below. Ready...and...

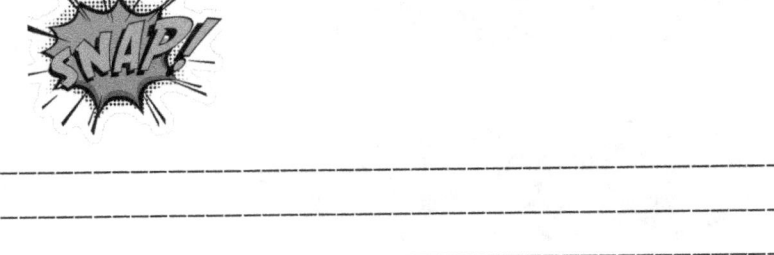

_____
_____
_____

CULTIVATION SCRAMBLE

Unscramble the words in the first row by connecting them with their match on the right.

STISAS	ENCOURAGE
FLUPIT	RELATIONSHIP
ERTURNU	GOODWILL
OPSUTRP	UPLIFT
CEENUOGAR	NURTURE
GOLLIWOD	ASSIST
HIPSTONIREAL	SUPPORT

DAY 3
Respect Personal Space

If you are highly social, you probably find it easy to make conversation. You float in and out of conversations with ease. But what if you're not that person? What if being physically near other people makes you anxious, so you're constantly looking for an exit plan? Perhaps you're one of the people who feels comfortable talking with others but prefers small gatherings. Regardless of where you land on the spectrum, respecting personal space is where we all need to gain insight and awareness.

Studies have been conducted that report we humans have a high percentage rate of non-verbal communication. Words are powerful, but they are not the only way to express ourselves. Body language and facial expression play a huge part too.

So, what are the social cues we need to pay attention to in order to respect someone's personal space? See if any of these hit home: (Check off the ones that stand out to you.)

☐ Tone of Voice	☐ Turns Shoulder Towards	☐ Proximity
☐ Minimal Eye Contact	☐ Crosses Arms	☐ Trembling Lips
☐ Hand Gestures	☐ Backs Away	☐ Laughter
☐ Tight, Pursed Lips	☐ Fidgets	☐ Grumbling
☐ Smile	☐ In Your Face	☐ Clenched Teeth
☐ Frown	☐ Mumbles	☐ Someone looking you in the eyes

Let's see how good you are at detecting social cues. How would you handle the following situations respectfully if they happened to you?

- Someone from school 'gets in your face.' What do you do?

_____

- Your friend is fidgeting right before a test. What do you say to her?

_____

- Your mom's lips are trembling, and tears are forming in her eyes. What do you do?

_____

- A boy at school is non-verbal, but he smiles at you. How do you respond?

_____

- You get super anxious when anyone moves too close to you. Imagine that now. How do you respond?

_____

- How do you respond when a sibling throws up her arms in reply to your comment as if to say, "What do you want *me* to do about it?"

_____

- Do you respond more positively when you're mad or when you're happy? Why or why not?

_____

CULTIVATION

WORD SEARCH

```
D N Z J H A N O R P Q S
E F Q K P C O U R A G E
P R O M O T E M B M Z D
E C H S U E B V C F U L
N B F O T H I N K E G A
D M N H A E F J U E R F
A N D R A X R Z C P O F
B W M O C M P A N K W E
I Q Z N R E R X M P T R
L L R I P B D E N O H D
I Q Z V M N B A K Q A R
T A K E O N Z M R I O P
Y L E S T Q D Z M N P A
```

DEPENDABILITY	PROMOTE	GROWTH
COURAGE	THINK	HONE
TAKE ON	FOSTER	EMBRACE

DAY 4

The Golden Rule

In the Bible, there is a scene called The Sermon on the Mount. Though the location isn't known precisely, the message Jesus communicated in that place is known around the globe. In the book of Matthew, in the scenario described in Chapters 5-7, Jesus gives a phenomenal speech about how to treat one another. But the most widely known passage is *Matthew 7:12*, which is recorded in the NIV with these words: "So in everything, do to others what you would have them do to you, for this sums up the Law and the Prophets." This is known as The Golden Rule.

The Golden Rule is good common sense, isn't it? If you want someone to be kind to you, be kind to them. If you want help cleaning your bedroom, help your sibling clean theirs. If you judge a schoolmate by their clothing, expect that you too, will be judged for yours. If you show respect to your family and friends, they are more likely to respect you. It's such a simple rule, but yet so powerful.

When you develop the Golden Rule in your life, you will cultivate strong relationships with your friends and family. If you have a lot of conflict in your relationships, fixing this will take time, energy, and self-control. Don't give up! I believe you can do this. You'll be setting such a great example for your siblings—and even your friends. In this season of cultivation, you will also learn patience. Everything worthwhile takes time.

Opposites

Draw a line between the left-hand and right-hand columns connecting the cultivation word with its opposite. Use a thesaurus if you'd like.

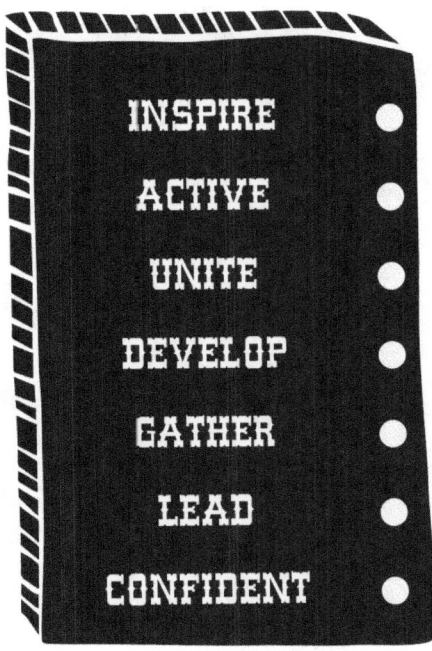

INSPIRE

ACTIVE

UNITE

DEVELOP

GATHER

LEAD

CONFIDENT

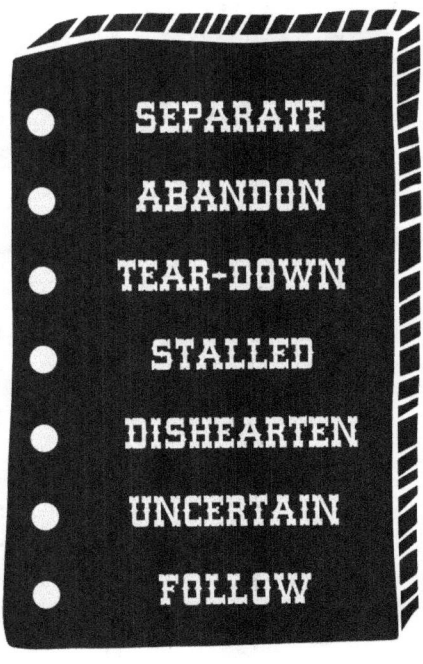

SEPARATE

ABANDON

TEAR-DOWN

STALLED

DISHEARTEN

UNCERTAIN

FOLLOW

CULTIVATION MAZE

Help KIM reach the key to cultivation.
Keep track of how many keys KIM has collected on page 125....

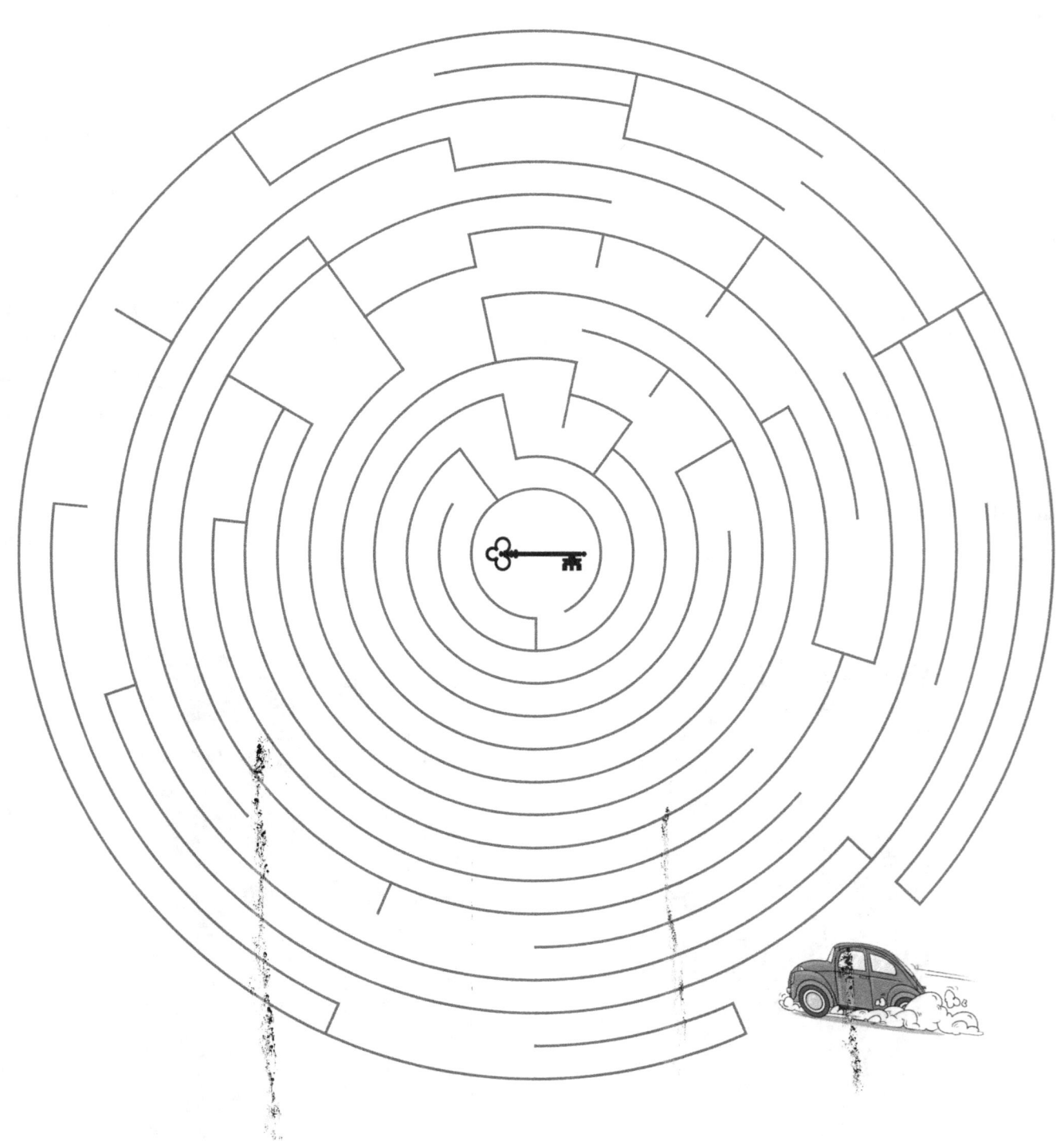

DAY 5

 Co-Pilot With God

Co-piloting with Dad in our airplane was a blast! I learned how to control the yoke and rudders to make the plane change direction. I could read the control panel to determine the elevation, speed, horizon, fuel level, and more. I also learned how to take off and land. You'd be right if you guessed that lancing was the scariest part. I wouldn't trade those days for anything! I was with my dad. He was my instructor and protector.

Co-piloting with God is similar to the experience I had flying with Dad. Can you imagine if I jumped into the pilot's seat and prepared for takeoff but expected Dad to only go along for the flight? I learned some basics of flying, but never enough to fly on my own. So, no. That wouldn't have been smart. God has so much to teach us.

The same goes for our relationship with God. He wants to be on our life journey with us. He wants to teach us how to take off and land without crashing. He will guide us in every aspect of our lives as he enables us to make decisions for ourselves along the way. At times it can be scary when you're close to 'touching down' for making a decision. He will never steer you wrong when you put your trust in Him.

Check the True or False box for each statement.

T   F

God is a gentle guide and strong protector.

Your journey is easier with God in the pilot's seat.

It's good to lead your friends into risky situations.

Selfish ways will surely make God happy.

Embracing meanness will cause you trouble.

Cultivating relationships will help you earn respect.

You will be more confident if you have self-respect.

CULTIVATION Code Breaker

Use the key below to break the code.

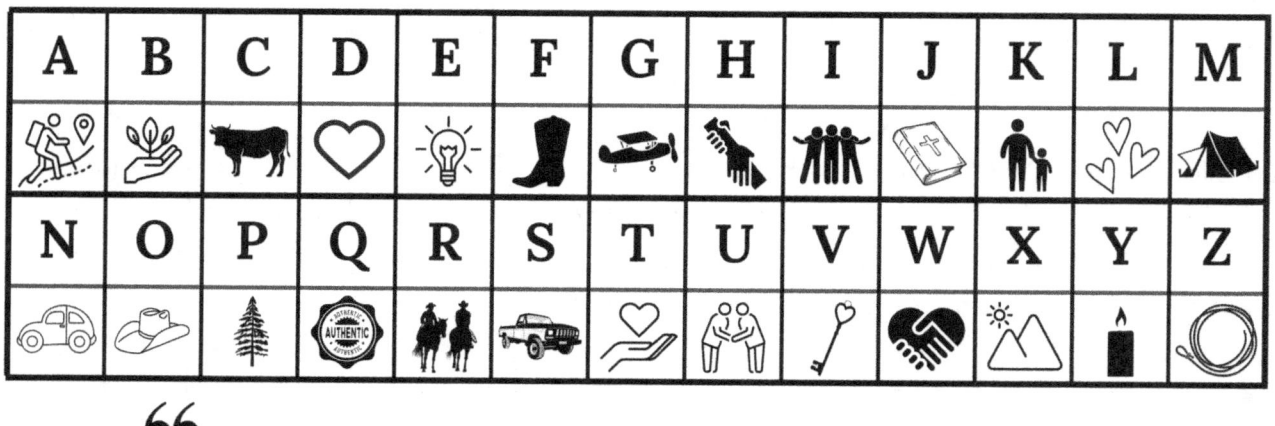

"ABOVE ALL,

LOVE EACH OTHER

DEEPLY, BECAUSE

LOVE COVERS OVER

A MULTITUDE"

OF SINS.

DAY 6
Stalled Out Thinking

Remember in the "Flying with Dad" story, where I explained how the airplane propeller stopped when Dad pointed the nose of the plane heavenward? As we ascended, we felt gravity slowing the aircraft until it was no longer gaining altitude. Then, Dad righted the plane's position to become horizontal again before turning the engine back on. The propeller thrust us onward. This action is called 'stalling out.'

Stalling out in Dad's airplane was an exhilarating experience. But stalling out in our thought processes... Not so much! Let's compare this analogy to situations in your life where your reasoning becomes flawed. You begin to choke and sputter while struggling with your identity and purpose. Much like the plane coming to a vertical position with the engine shut down, you become sluggish in your desire to do the right thing. We've all been there!

Making wise choices will be a daily decision. There's no time for slack-mindedness. You were designed for a great purpose. That entails turning your thought engine back on and moving forward with intention. I love the Message translation in *Ephesians 6:13-18* regarding God's armor: "Be prepared. You're up against far more than you can handle on your own. Take all the help you can get, every weapon God has issued, so that when it's all over but the shouting you'll still be on your feet. Truth, righteousness, peace, faith, and salvation are more than words. Learn how to apply them. You'll need them throughout your life. God's Word is an indispensable weapon. In the same way, prayer is essential in this ongoing warfare. Pray hard and long. Pray for your brothers and sisters. Keep your eyes open. Keep each other's spirits up so that no one falls behind or drops out."

 **REFLECTION TIME**

How does it make you feel when you fall behind in your schoolwork?

Frustrated? ____ Angry? ____ Complacent? ____ Anxious? ____ Fearful? ____

If you are able to make it up, write one positive step you can take to catch up on your work.

_____

How do you react when learning a fairly simple new skill?

Positive? ____ Negative? ____ Neutral? ____

If learning the new skill was intimidating, would you still give the same answer?

Yes? ____ No? ____

If you answered no, explain how you might turn the experience into a positive one.

_____

How do you feel when you hear someone trash-talk another person?

Positive? ____ Negative? ____ Neutral? ____

Do you think this behavior is constructive? Yes? ____ No? ____ Why or why not?

_____

CULTIVATION

Self Evaluation Worksheet

Check the boxes that are true for you.

I can...	I can do this very well	I can do this fairly well	I can do this with some help	I need more practice
Stand for what is right				
Choose peace over conflict				
Respect personal space				
Honor the golden rule				
Change my stalled out thinking				
Recognize and respect differences				

Complete the table below.

I can cultivate relationships by	
One thing I need to improve	
To improve I can	
One way to respect personal space	

DAY 7

Recognize and Respect Differences

Winnie The Pooh said, "The things that make me different are the things that make me." Pooh understood that he was unique. He loved his friends and his honey, didn't he?

You might ask me, "What is unique about *you*?" Well, I see myself as a fair-skinned middle-aged woman of average height—a little chubby and requiring eyeglasses."But," you say, "That's just what you look like on the *outside*. What makes your personality unique?"

I answer: "Now you've got me thinking. *Hmm*...I enjoy writing, nature walks, cooking, and time with my family. But I guess if you're asking what is unique to me, I'd have to say kindness and empathy toward others.

Now it's *your* turn. What about you and *your* uniqueness? Name something classic most people know about you. _____ Now, write something about you that is one-of-a-kind. _____ Is this something you possess that you could gift to someone else (For example: time, skill, or ability)? If so, write it here.

_____

We all need to work diligently toward recognizing and respecting the differences in others. Limiting our beliefs about ourselves and others impairs us all. Speaking specifically about color, I absolutely love Crayola crayons. I have never outgrown the joy of coloring. My newest favorites are the skin-colored ones. Coloring with them acknowledges that we are not simply red, yellow, black, and white humans but every variety and shade of skin color. That's the creativity of our Master Designer. We have so much to learn about one another.

In this key for cultivating good relationships, think about someone you know at church, club, or school who is different from you in some way. Let's say you would like to get to know them better. What can you say or do to start a conversation with them?

_____

_____

Now, someone wants to know you better. What are three questions you'd like someone to ask you about your uniqueness? _____

_____

Accept awkwardness. Quite often, people don't know what words to say. What social cues would you give to put someone at ease around you? _____

What words could you say to make them comfortable? _____

_____

CULTIVATION KEY

How well do you cultivate? Circle the best answer for each scenario.

1. There is a new kid in school. Do you...

Welcome them and try to get to know them.	Talk behind their back.	Ignore them.	Make fun of them.
A	B	C	D

2. Your teacher asks you to do something that takes great courage. Do you...

Say, "No, thank you. I am not brave."	Say, "I'm nervous but I'll give it a try."	Think you might be called the teacher's pet if you do it.	Ignore the opportunity.
A	B	C	D

3. You're running for class president. Do you...

Listen to classmates ideas to make your school better.	Think you know best without the classmates input, so you don't ask.	Talk disrespectfully about your competitors.	Figure you can get elected with your good looks.
A	B	C	D

4. Your sibling yells at you. Do you...

Ignore them.	Yell back.	Ask them how you can resolve the issue, calmly.	Tattle on them.
A	B	C	D

5. You just got hired for your first job pet sitting. Do you...

Act dependably, show up on time, and take care of the pets.	Fail to show up.	Show up but play on your phone instead of taking care of the pets.	Show up thirty minutes late without calling.
A	B	C	D

6. Your friend tells you a non-harmful secret and asks you not to tell anyone. Do you...

Shout her secret from the rooftop.	Tell her you won't tell anyone but do tell a friend that tells another friend and so on.	Judge your friend unfairy for what she confided in you.	Keep your promise not to tell.
A	B	C	D

Talk about your answers with a parent, grandparent, or mentor.

CULTIVATION
QUIZ KEY

On the Cultivation quiz page, you circled A, B, C or D for each scenario.

You can see below that each letter is = to a number from 0 to 3

In the 'Points' box, write the number = to the letter
you circled for each scenario in the quiz.

Next, add the numbers together at the bottom for your total.

Points

1. A=3 B=2 C=1 D=0

2. A=2 B=3 C=1 D=0

3. A=3 B=2 C=0 D=1

4. A=0 B=2 C=3 D=1

5. A=3 B=1 C=0 D=2

6. A=0 B=1 C=2 D=3

+ _____

Next, write your total from this page in the Cultivation
box on page 123 to calculate your overall score.

Total

love

GENEROSITY

Dad and me, family reunion, 2011

> "Do all the good you can, by all the means you can, in all the ways you can, in all the places you can, at all the times you can, to all the people you can, as long as ever you can.
>
> John Wesley"

GENEROSITY

Love Bound in a T-Shirt

Dad's standards for living a good life were simple: Provide for your family's needs, love and support them through their challenges and accomplishments, and give generously to those in need. Dad had exciting hobbies he enjoyed throughout his lifetime, but they came second to the needs of others. If he was lending a hand to a neighbor, working to better church facilities, or simply holding a door for a passer-by, it was always with someone else's needs in mind.

There were some lean times during the years I was growing up. But somehow, we always had what we needed. Occasionally, Dad hunted and brought home wild game to help meet the family budget. Momma was a genius for making a thrifty meal taste like a gourmet banquet. Occasionally, Dad would surprise us with a drive-through ice cream cone on an otherwise uninspiring Sunday afternoon. It was rare that we ever ate out. But when we did, Dad always paid the tab, no matter who shared our table. It was not out of obligation. He was a giving man.

A great example of Dad's generosity is in a sweet, touching memory and life lesson I have always cherished. You may have heard the common saying, "He would give you the shirt off his back," indicating a valuable sacrifice that would greatly benefit another. This gift of time or resources shows respect and is considered an act of kindness. In other words, generosity is kindness in motion!

At the time, I was a young woman in my mid-twenties, married with two children. My folks were excited to see us all—especially the grandkids. Dad and Mom had traveled across three states to visit us at our home in Houston, Texas. A long time had passed since last I'd seen them. It seemed an eternity. I was so excited anticipating the time we'd share catching up on each other's lives. This was before cell phones and social media started making it easier to communicate.

Smiles and happy tears flooded our faces as we embraced. I wrapped my arms around my dad for a big hug and noticed how comfortable his shirt felt. It was a sporty, soft white T-shirt that had a yoke across the front, a rounded neck, and long sleeves. The double-knit indicated good-quality fabric. The special feature of that T-shirt was how it felt when blended with the love Dad poured into that long-overdue hug. He just smiled when I told him how much I loved his shirt.

We welcomed my folks into our home. Throughout our visit that day, I complimented Dad on how handsome he looked in the shirt—and just how cozy it felt to the touch. I commented on the shirt one last time, not realizing how much I'd gone on about it. Then something remarkable happened. Dad took off the shirt right where we stood, leaving his torso covered with an everyday T-shirt. My cheeks flushed awkwardly from embarrassment. My feelings must have been obvious. Dad folded the gift, still warm from his body, lifted my hands into a receiving position, and lovingly placed the shirt in them.

I stammered, trying to refuse the gift. Mortification set in hard and fast as I realized I had voiced my fondness for the shirt too much. Dad must have felt obliged to give it to me. But that's not how it happened. He just smiled those loving eyes of his and said, "No. You like it. I want you to have it." I was on the verge of missing the life lesson of Dad's generosity as kindness in motion. He wasn't giving to earn God's or man's attention. Nor out of the fear that I wouldn't love him if he didn't give it to me. And he wasn't giving the gift to get something in return. No, these were never Dad's motives. It was not for the fanfare or fame. It was not to make him feel superior. He expected nothing in return. It was a simple gift from a dad to his daughter with no strings attached. He was simply a generous man. Dad's love for his family and friends was straightforward. There was no hidden agenda. He gave what he had to make people's lives a little sweeter.

DAY 1

Be A Good Neighbor

"All of us, at some time or other, need help. Whether we're giving or receiving help, each one of us has something valuable to bring to this world." Fred Rogers spoke simple truths with such care and love for everyone. His PBS television series, Mister Rogers' Neighborhood, ran for thirty-three years. His considerate way of communicating demonstrated that being neighborly resonated with many generations of viewers. He honestly valued others and offered kindness and respect to everyone he met.

Using Mister Rogers as an example, let's consider some ways we can be neighborly. I'll list a few examples. Then, you can brainstorm ways you could make a difference in your own neighborhood. Jot them down.

- Has your neighbor been in the hospital? Maybe you could help your family make a home-cooked meal to take to them.
- Offer to pick up loose tree limbs or rake leaves in your neighbor's yard.
- Do you have an elderly neighbor? I bet they have stories they would like to share with you from their life experiences.
- Do they have a pet you could take care of while they are away?
- Pray for them.

Jot your ideas down now. Think of ways specific to your neighborhood where you could be generous. _____
_____
_____

Color the picture below. As you do, be mindful as you consider ways to be generous.

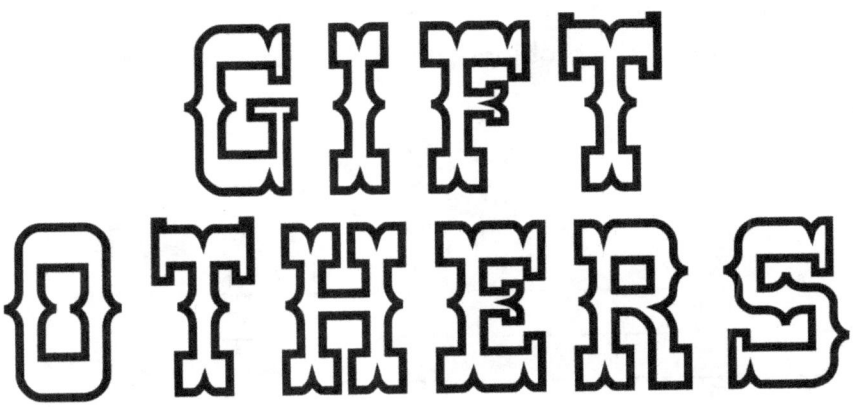

DAY 2

Lend A Hand

The subject of our study today goes beyond being neighborly. Lending a hand is something you can do just about anywhere. I love this scripture in *James*: Chapter *2:15-16* NIV reads, "Suppose a brother or a sister is without clothes and daily food. If one of you says to them, "Go in peace; keep warm and well fed," but does nothing about their physical needs, what good is it?" To paraphrase: don't use empty words saying you'll be generous and help while you have no intention of helping. Instead, be true to your word and give of yourself wholeheartedly when you offer to lend a hand. It's another way of boosting respect.

You've probably heard that it's better to give than to receive. It seems like a strange concept when you're young—because you're accustomed to receiving everything from your parents, grandparents, and teachers. But I want to challenge you to generously give of yourself in a way you have never experienced. It brings so much joy when you give to someone without expecting anything in return.

By all means, be generous with your time. With your parent's permission, volunteer at an animal shelter or food pantry. Offer something specific, like helping someone who fell get themselves back up. Compliment someone because you like their smile. Perform some small act of kindness, like making a cup of tea for your momma or handing your dad a tool when he's working on a project.

Turn This Scene Around

Ebenezer Scrooge is a selfish and stingy older man in Charles Dickens' book, *A Christmas Carol*. At this moment, you are acting just like Ebenezer before he transforms his character into a kindly, generous man. You've manipulated your sister into giving you her allowance. You walk away laughing, and your sister begins to cry.

Now, when I snap my finger, your attitude changes from selfish and greedy to kind and generous. How will you address the problem? How does the transformation feel?
Explain below. Ready...and...

_____

_____

_____

GENEROSITY SCRAMBLE

Unscramble the words in the first row by connecting them with their match on the right.

MUFLCREI	OFFER
SGODNESO	MERCIFUL
ELUPFHL	SHARE
REFOF	GOODNESS
VLEO	HELPFUL
RAHES	LOVE
BDANTUNA	ABUNDANT

DAY 3

Selflessness

Would it be easier to climb to the top of a snow-filled mountain or ski down from the top to the bottom? The path of least resistance is the perceived easier route, isn't it? Though selflessness is not like climbing up to a mountaintop, it certainly takes more effort in the beginning to create a daily habit of thinking more about others.

When we are so consumed by our own issues, we don't use our wide lens of focus to observe the needs of our friends and family. We are only motivated by what we want, like a new toy. But what if we could turn that around? What if you started by making a list of every toy in your bedroom? How long would your list be? It's common to find lost toys under the bed, closet, drawers, and toybox. Like clothes in the closet, you probably have much more clothing than you can wear in any given week.

Here's a great Scripture reference for you to keep in mind: "Do everything readily and cheerfully—no bickering, no second-guessing allowed! Go out into the world uncorrupted, a breath of fresh air in this squalid and polluted society. Provide people with a glimpse of good living and of the living God. Carry the light-giving Message into the night so I'll have good cause to be proud of you on the day that Christ returns" (*Philippians 2:14-15 MSG*).

What would your room look like if you donated the toys you don't play with and the clothes you don't wear? It would look less cluttered, for sure. And honestly, less is more. It is a generous gesture when you begin to connect with others by sharing what you have. But that's not all. A minimalist attitude also gives you inner joy because your wide lens of generosity is now focused on what matters: Being selfless.

- List five objects you own right now that you can either give to a friend in need or donate to charity. _____
- List five items of clothing (still in good, wearable condition) that you could share with a friend in need or donate to charity. _____
- Do you have a favorite ball cap, book, or collectible you could gift to a friend? Think of something you could offer to brighten a friend's day._____
- Does your school have a coat drive where you can donate your outgrown coat to someone who might otherwise not have one? _____
- Think of other ways to be generous with your time or belongings. List at least one generous thing you can do today. _____

GENEROSITY

WORD SEARCH

```
E B F D S T U O I M N X
P I I T A W D E R P O Z
O G Y R W N Q U I L X N
C H A R I T A B L E H A
B E M K X G N W E R S I
G A H Q P N S N T F I G
S R V M O I W E R O F P
F T I A M V E B V C L P
G E N E R O U S S U E Y
N D M X I L L A T Y S Q
V K L S H A R E O Z N B
P O I Q A C V E G H U Q
F R E E G I V I N G M S
```

BIG HEARTED	UNSELFISH	CHARITABLE
FREE GIVING	SHARE	KIND
GIFT	GENEROUS	LOVING

DAY 4

Kindness in Motion

Does the fact that Dad didn't have to buy the T-shirt for me lead you to believe it meant less to him to gift—or for me to receive it? Not at all. Cost isn't always a factor in giving. Kindness in motion is a way to express love through your gift of time or possessions in an ongoing way. It is not something you do once, check it off your bucket list, and go on with your life. No, it's something you do as you go through each day, broadening your scope of vision and keep on finding new ways to show you care about others.

Let's look at this simple example of kindness in motion: You are tagging behind Mom in the grocery store. You notice a woman in a wheelchair reaching toward a shelf she can't quite reach. Instead of ignoring her, you offer to get the grocery item for her.

Extraordinary occasions occur when kindness and generosity become part of your regular mindset. These virtues are contagious. Unlike a pandemic, kindness and generosity bring people together. Smiles begin to appear regularly. Inspiration to go outside our everyday thinking and create kind-hearted realities can make people's lives a little better. In some way, you have been given a gift. Now it's your turn to bless others.

Opposites

Draw a line between the left-hand and right-hand columns connecting the generosity word with its opposite. Use a thesaurus if you'd like.

GENTLE
SELFLESS
CHARITABLE
THOUGHTFUL
OFFER
PLENTIFUL
GIVE

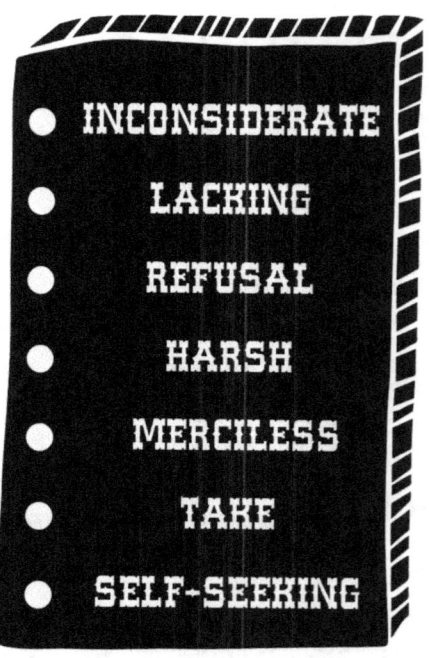

INCONSIDERATE
LACKING
REFUSAL
HARSH
MERCILESS
TAKE
SELF-SEEKING

GENEROSITY MAZE

Help KIM reach the key to cultivation.
Keep track of how many keys KIM has collected on page 125....

DAY 5

Pay It Forward

Does the idiom "no strings attached" sound familiar to you? As far back as the 18th century, fabric merchants tied strings onto the visible flaws in the fabric they weaved. When a customer wanted to purchase a flawless piece of cloth, they would ask for one without strings attached. In other words, the customer was not obliged to buy the defective parts. Today, it means no obligation or condition in which one must be repaid. In other words: Pay it forward. When you do this act of kindness, you extend generosity to someone else the next time. You do it for kindness' sake.

Proverbs 11:25 MSG reads, "The one who blesses others is abundantly blessed; those who help others are helped." The cool thing about blessing others is that 1) It does your heart good, and 2) Paying it forward is ongoing. That's the whole idea behind it. It's the gift that keeps on giving.

Even something as simple as a smile could brighten another person's day as a special gift. Then they, in turn, could pass on that smile to someone else. Have you been able to pay anything forward? If yes, could you write it here? _____
If not, write something you could pay forward: _____

Check the True or False box for each statement.

	T	F
Generosity means self-seeking.	☐	☐
A smile could lift someone's sadness.	☐	☐
Kindness is a strength.	☐	☐
Doing things without obligation is a good thing.	☐	☐
To give and expect something in return is advised.	☐	☐
There are countless ways to pay it forward.	☐	☐
It is more blessed to give than receive.	☐	☐

GENEROSITY Code Breaker

Use the key below to break the code.

A	B	C	D	E	F	G	H	I	J	K	L	M
N	O	P	Q	R	S	T	U	V	W	X	Y	Z

"

FOR WHERE

YOUR TREASURE

IS, THERE YOUR

HEART WILL

"

BE ALSO.

83

DAY 6
Give Without Fanfare or Fame

Have you ever watched a quarterback in a football game when he makes a touchdown? The crowd goes wild with cheers as the player does a wonky dance and slams the ball down. He's showing off. It's all part of the thrill of the game. All eyes are on him. He's the star.

As I mentioned in the story this week, there was not a big crowd of witnesses around when Dad handed me the T-shirt. In fact, Mom and I may have been the only ones who noticed. Granted, Dad was not a superstar like the ones people pay good money to see. But Dad did have a superpower: It was love displayed through generous acts of kindness.

There is a great scripture that confirms this way of thinking. It's found in Matthew 6:2-4 MSG, "When you do something for someone else, don't call attention to yourself. You've seen them in action, I'm sure—'playactors' I call them—treating prayer meeting and street corner alike as a stage, acting compassionate as long as someone is watching, playing to the crowds. They get applause, true, but that's all they get. When you help someone out, don't think about how it looks. Just do it—quietly and unobtrusively. That is the way your God, who conceived you in love, working behind the scenes, helps you out."

 **REFLECTION TIME**

How would you feel if someone paid your late fee at the library without you knowing?
Would you be Happy?__ Embarrassed?__ Thankful?__ Sad?__ Wouldn't Care?__

If you had the money and paid for the meal of the person in line behind you, how do you think that person would feel?
Joyful?____ Angry?____ Wouldn't Care?____.
If you chose "angry," why do you think that would be?_____

Imagine someone sending you a greeting card through the mail.
Would you feel Light-Hearted?____ Excited?____ Joyful?____ it Doesn't Matter?____

Imagine that you color or draw a picture, roll it up, tie it with a ribbon, and leave it at a neighbor's door as a gift. How do you think your neighbor will respond to this kindness?
Sad?____ Surprised?____ Joyful?____ Amazed?____ Won't Care?____

You did a thoughtful thing by sending your mentor a letter to let them know you're thinking about and appreciate them. How do you think your mentor will respond?
Happy?____ Sad?____ Responsive?____ Won't Care?____

GENEROSITY
Self Evaluation Worksheet

Check the boxes that are true for you.

I can...	I can do this very well	I can do this fairly well	I can do this with some help	I need more practice
Be a good neighbor				
Lend a hand				
Be kindness in motion				
Pay it forward				
Give without fanfare or notoriety				
Expect nothing in return				

Complete the table below.

I can be generous by	
One thing I need to improve	
To improve I can	
One way to pay it forward	

DAY 7
Expect Nothing In Return

The big takeaway in the generosity key is that we want to give wholeheartedly to people to awaken the joy in their lives. My dad taught us that generosity could be as simple as giving someone an unexpected gift. Sometimes, the trouble begins when one assumes they should get something in return for the kindness. A good quote you can remember from Wayne Dyer is: "Anonymously perform acts of kindness, expecting nothing in return—not even a 'thank you.'

We should never expect something in return for the kindness we extend to others. *Luke 6:35-36* MSG reads, "I tell you, love your enemies. Help and give without expecting a return. You'll never—I promise—regret it. Live out this God-created identity the way our Father lives toward us, generously and graciously, even when we're at our worst. Our Father is kind; you be kind."

It may seem odd not to expect even a 'thank you.' After all, it's common courtesy to say "Thanks." The point here is that you are giving for the sake of giving. Your mind will be free of tension if you aren't concerned with getting something out of the deal. By and by, with this practice, you will find even more opportunities to give selflessly. And it's a good feeling, 'to boot.'

Kindness is Free

What percentage are you willing to give of yourself when you see someone in need? Put a check next to your answer. 10%_ 20%_ 30%_ 40%_ 50%_ 60%_ 70%_ 80%_ 90%_ 100%_

Now, answer the same question, but this time you are faced with helping an elderly person cross the road. What percentage are you willing to give of yourself in that situation?
10%_ 20%_ 30%_ 40%_ 50%_ 60%_ 70%_ 80%_ 90%_ 100%_

Consider the same original question, but this time you are faced with helping a neighbor with their yard work. What percentage are you willing to give of yourself in that situation?
10%_ 20%_ 30%_ 40%_ 50%_ 60%_ 70%_ 80%_ 90%_ 100%_

Consider the same original question, but this time you are faced with doing the dishes without being asked. What percentage are you willing to give of yourself in that situation?
10%_ 20%_ 30%_ 40%_ 50%_ 60%_ 70%_ 80%_ 90%_ 100%_

How did your percentages compare? Were you more willing to be generous when the job was easy? Take some time today to consider new ways to grant the gift of giving. Generosity comes from the heart—and for the benefit of others.

GENEROSITY KEY

How generous are you? Circle the best answer for each scenario.

1. You earned an extra $10 for going above and beyond what was expected. Do

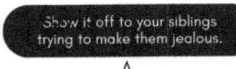
Show it off to your siblings trying to make them jealous.
A

Boast about it at school.
B

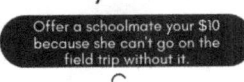
Offer a schoolmate your $10 because she can't go on the field trip without it.
C

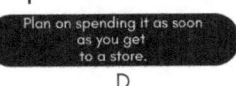
Plan on spending it as soon as you get to a store.
D

2. You have a room full of games and toys. Do you...

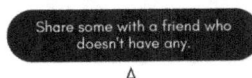
Share some with a friend who doesn't have any.
A

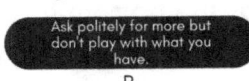
Ask politely for more but don't play with what you have.
B

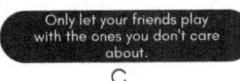
Only let your friends play with the ones you don't care about.
C

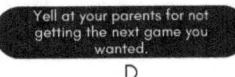
Yell at your parents for not getting the next game you wanted.
D

3. Someone falls. Do you...

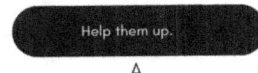
Help them up.
A

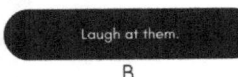
Laugh at them.
B

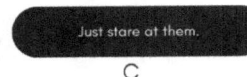
Just stare at them.
C

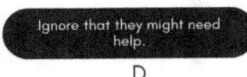
Ignore that they might need help.
D

4. A frail, elderly woman is looking for a chair, but they are all occupied. Do you...

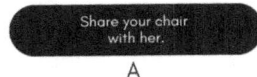
Share your chair with her.
A

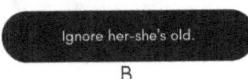
Ignore her-she's old.
B

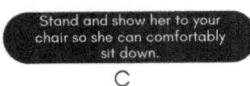
Stand and show her to your chair so she can comfortably sit down.
C

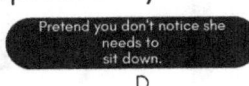
Pretend you don't notice she needs to sit down.
D

5. Your youth pastor has asked for your help at Harvest Fest. Do you...

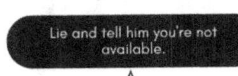
Lie and tell him you're not available.
A

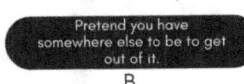
Pretend you have somewhere else to be to get out of it.
B

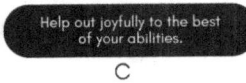
Help out joyfully to the best of your abilities.
C

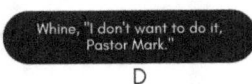
Whine, "I don't want to do it, Pastor Mark."
D

6. You have some extra time this weekend. Do you...

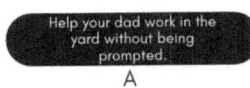
Help your dad work in the yard without being prompted.
A

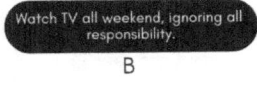
Watch TV all weekend, ignoring all responsibility.
B

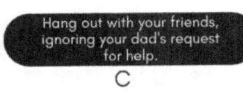
Hang out with your friends, ignoring your dad's request for help.
C

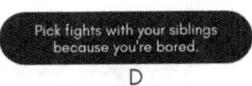
Pick fights with your siblings because you're bored.
D

Talk about your answers with a parent, grandparent, or mentor.

GENEROSITY
QUIZ KEY

On the Generosity quiz page, you circled A, B, C or D for each scenario.

You can see below that each letter is = to a number from 0 to 3

In the 'Points' box, write the number = to the letter
you circled for each scenario in the quiz.

Next, add the numbers together at the bottom for your total.

1. A=1 B=0 C=3 D=2

2. A=3 B=2 C=1 D=0

3. A=3 B=1 C=2 D=0

4. A=2 B=1 C=3 D=1

5. A=0 B=1 C=3 D=2

6. A=3 B=1 C=2 D=0

Points

+ _____

Next, write your total from this page in the Generosity
box on page 123 to calculate your overall score.

Total

88

Dad in Flastaff, AZ

Senior year of high school

The day Dad became an ordained deacon

ORDINATION

DEACON

Loving father

HUMILITY

> "Greatness is not found in possessions, power, position, or prestige. It is discovered in goodness, humility, service, and character."
> William Arthur Ward

HUMILITY

A Servant's Heart

His weathered and aged hands reflected a lifetime of servanthood. Wrinkles brought on by multiple years on this earth, along with callouses and stiffness, were tell-tale signs that the man had worked a lot. We sat together in the sunroom on this ordinary visit to their cabin in the woods. I noticed Dad's hands as he chorded a few songs on the guitar. I began to ponder how he had touched others' lives for the good. Raised by parents who modeled humility, it was a given. He knew if a neighbor, stranger, or family member was in need, he did what he could to help: Always giving—never asking for anything in return.

Taking a step of faith in the summer of 1956, Dad decided to get baptized into the family of God. It was most natural for this young cowboy to get baptized in a stock tank used for watering cattle. Like many new to the church, Dad thought it was a place where good folks worshiped. It wasn't long before he witnessed a scene where his momma was told she was not welcome at a church she tried to attend. He thought if that church wasn't good enough for his momma, it sure wasn't good enough for him. The duplicity both angered and disillusioned him. For the next fifty years, Dad only attended church for weddings and funerals.

With property purchased from Mom's uncle, my folks moved from Arizona to a hemmed-in hollow in the woods of Arkansas, better known as God's Country. The green grass, sparkling rivers, rolling hills, friendly people—and trees of all kinds that produce beautiful autumns—made this area a nice place to retire. A new beginning in this small community was just what the Holy Spirit had in mind. He planted one tiny mustard seed of truth that made Dad re-examine his walk with the Lord. Mom's joy overflowed when Dad accepted her invitation to attend church just down the road.

Dad soon found he belonged there. It wasn't long before the church members realized what a treasure of a man had walked through those doors. Sunday mornings, Dad, known as Buzz to family and friends, arrived early to make coffee for the men. He looked forward to talking with them before the morning service about all things: hunting, fishing, and business. He had a way of making each person feel important simply by being a good listener and putting their concerns above his own.

On January 3, 2010, Dad and Mom re-dedicated their lives to the Lord Jesus through baptism. The pastor and elders began to call on Dad for congregational prayers, carrying offering baskets, and joining the worship team. Of course, music had always been a joy for him. So, that was an easy fit. With Dad on his guitar and Mom with her mandolin, they added harmoniously to the little country church.

Dad enjoyed fellowship with the members. He realized they were people just like him, in need of a Savior—and that church was for those seeking to grow closer to God despite their shortcomings. This new perspective gave Dad a level of insight he'd never known.

But that wasn't all Dad accomplished there. He was also called upon for repairs, construction, and cemetery duties. The body of a church has many moving parts. To make it work successfully, everyone must work together. Dad understood that he was now part of an eternal family—not just an earthly church.

Early on, Dad didn't feel qualified to lead or teach. He convinced himself there were others much more learned than he. But eventually, he was called on and did teach. Scripture speaks of the weight of a teacher's position. Dad took this calling seriously. He researched well, bringing maps and study guides to make his lessons lively. When Dad taught, the members thoroughly enjoyed participating in the Sunday School classes.

Dad fashioned his life as a man after God's own heart, but he never imagined himself as a church leader. Nonetheless, the deacons saw integrity, reverence, and humility in Dad's demeanor. They knew he would be a great fit as a deacon and were determined to proceed with the request. But Dad declined the invitation twice.

In his formative years, Dad had seen how church politics caused harm. Also, he was just a member who liked to serve. Surely this deacon business was not for him. But they told him, "We sure would like you to join us as a deacon, Buzz. We hope you'll reconsider."

Dad never jumped blindly into any project or task. He took this one to the Lord in prayer. The third time he was invited, he spoke humbly: "Well, if that's what the church family wants, I'll do it. I'd be honored."

There was hardly a dry eye in the church when Dad was ordained. Family and friends witnessed something truly unique. A gentle, unassuming man with willing hands, who everyone loved, settled into a position of leadership unlike anything he'd ever expected to do in his life.

God called. Dad humbly accepted. This obedience set a generational example throughout his earthly family that would have eternal consequences.

DAY 1

Consider Others First

Humility is a virtue that makes us profoundly conscious of the world around us. It makes us take into account our actions, body language, and speech toward others. It also makes us critically aware of our belonging, but it doesn't take away from our being.

The example Dad sets in the story, 'A Servant's Heart' exemplifies the virtue of humility. And it is a way of life. It's how a person takes on every challenge, conversation, and thought. Considering others first doesn't come naturally to most of us, though it *is* feasible. Typically, people look out for themselves (referred to as looking out for "Number One"). Ultimately, we do it because we're in survival mode. But for today's exercise, I want you, the reader, to think outside the mentality of Self.

Do nothing out of selfish ambition or vain conceit.
Rather, in humility value others above yourselves" (*Philippians 2:3* NIV).

The call for Dad to devote his life to serving the church as a deacon put him in the position of shepherding the people. This meant that, at times, he put the needs of the church above his own. Examples of this include hospital visits to a church member in need, welcoming visitors to the church service, and maintaining the church grounds. Of course, he still had his responsibilities at home. But, wherever he saw a need, he made it a priority to consider others first.

Try to consider others first as you go through your week. Remember that Jesus set an example for having the most incredible humility. He accepted the call to redeem our shortcomings and bridge the gap between our sins and God's perfect and pure majesty. That's the highest level of consideration for others.

Color the picture below. As you do, be mindful as you consider ways to put others first.

DAY 2

Walk A Mile In Their Shoes

Here's a fun fact: During Jesus' ministry, he walked over three thousand miles. There are approximately two thousand five hundred steps in a mile. Doing the math, it totals roughly seven million five hundred thousand steps that Jesus walked in three years. Can you imagine walking alongside him and being mentored by the greatest mentor of all time? And yet, not one of his disciples could wear Jesus' shoes. It wasn't because they were the wrong size, but because they believed Jesus was the only one who could redeem the world.

It's easy to judge another person based on our perception of a situation. Generally, though, we don't take the time to visualize ourselves in that same circumstance. So, is it fair to cast judgment without first considering what a person has gone through?

If you haven't had the opportunity to read To Kill a Mockingbird yet, there are a few memorable lines that the main character, Atticus, shares with his daughter, Scout: "If you can learn a simple trick, Scout, you'll get along a lot better with all kinds of folks. You never really understand a person until you consider things from his point of view, until you climb inside of his skin and walk around in it."

Often, people judge harshly to keep the critical finger from being pointed back toward them. Judging someone else can even help them justify their own harmful motives. Imagine walking the same road as the person you're thinking of criticizing. Perception is everything! Consider the other person your equal rather than someone inferior to you. With this mindset, you'll most certainly improve your relationships and gain more friends.

Turn This Scene Around

Charlie sits next to you in class. Though you have no idea why and haven't cared to ask, you blurt out, "Man, you stink! Don't you ever take a shower?" The class snickers at your bold and disrespectful comment. Charlie's family has money problems right now because of his mom's medical bills. So, they got their water turned off last week. That's why he hasn't taken a shower lately.

Now, when I snap my fingers, you've talked with Charlie privately. How do you address the clarified situation? Explain below.
Ready...and...

_____

_____

HUMILITY SCRAMBLE

Unscramble the words in the first row by connecting them with their match on the right.

TAPENIT	MEEKNESS
FUTIDUL	RESERVED
VEDRERES	PATIENT
TENPRESUOITUN	OBEDIENT
DEOTIBNE	DUTIFUL
SMEKSNEE	UNASSUMING
SANUMSIGNU	UNPRETENTIOUS

DAY 3

Tame The Tongue~Words Matter

Have you ever watched any of the old television westerns? Like most good story plots, there would be a leading man usually wearing a white hat to represent an upright and moral character. To add conflict, a black-hatted villain would represent evil. The hero with the white hat stood for honor, honesty, and justice. And the villain stood for disrespect, deceit, and corruption.

Just like the contrast between the hero and the villain, our tongues communicate our words for both good and evil. Our God-given free will allows us to choose how we use our tongues. There are more than a hundred references in the Bible about the tongue. Don't you think God is trying to make a point? One reference comes from *James 3:9-12* CEV, "My dear friends, with our tongues we speak both praises and curses. We praise our Lord and Father, and we curse people who were created to be like God, and this isn't right. Can clean water and dirty water both flow from the same spring? Can a fig tree produce olives or a grapevine produce figs? Does fresh water come from a well full of salt water?"

One of the emperors of Rome, Marcus Aurelius, also had some excellent advice about the tongue: "Whenever you are about to find fault with someone, ask yourself the following question: What fault of mine most nearly resembles the one I am about to criticize?" It's good advice because it turns the mirror back on ourselves, causing us to consider the motives that guide us.

As a people, we have grown lazy about healthy communication in this 'internet age.' We can bash other people's beliefs, appearances, race—you name it—all behind the curtain of the computer screen. We use words that probably wouldn't have been used had we been talking face-to-face. It's time to make a difference! Use your words to uplift others rather than tearing them down. Think of ways to encourage others and speak words that inspire them.

- Why do you think the tongue is talked about so much in the bible? _____
_____
- We should be conscious of the words we use when speaking. Why? _____
_____
- Why is it important to speak words of inspiration, comfort, and encouragement? _____
_____
- Name something you can do to 'put the kibosh' on complaining. _____
_____
- How can you be the hero instead of the villain of your life story? _____
_____
- Can you ask God to help you use your words to uplift others? _____
_____

HUMILITY

WORD SEARCH

```
B O H P B K L A N V A L
M E P L X C K A E O T D
E I N T E G R I T Y W H
E R S T Y Q U Z S Q A T
K V I E M N I W I A E R
N H O P G E N T L E Q A
E S E T C X A S L T E E
S C B L N Q A B H K P O
S G J O P A M O D E S T
T R A W E U L K A Y W N
W O P D H A S F G H L W
T S U O E T R U O C A O
A W T E N M U H J K L D
```

HELP	COURTEOUS	MEEKNESS
GENTLE	DOWN-TO-EARTH	MODEST
HUMBLE	LISTEN	INTEGRITY

DAY 4

Forgive And Love Much

This is a difficult lesson. When someone wrongs you, is your first response to forgive? No. Generally, human nature tends to want to pay back the wrongdoing with more wrongdoings. You hurt someone that hurt you. You lash out in your defense to claim your victory in a dispute. But this only fans the flame of discontentment. It does nothing to resolve the turmoil of the conflict. Forgiving others is one of the most challenging lessons in life for everyone.

So, how do we go about forgiving someone? The short answer is LOVE. My favorite scripture regarding love is *1 Corinthians 13:4-7* ESV: "Love is patient and kind; love does not envy or boast; it is not arrogant or rude. It does not insist on its own way; it is not irritable or resentful; it does not rejoice at wrongdoing, but rejoices with the truth. Love bears all things, believes all things, hopes all things, and endures all things."

Breaking down the components of that scripture gives you everything you need to forgive others. Throw envy, resentment, arrogance, and disrespectful attitudes out the window. Embrace love instead. As you let go of every hurt, you will begin to feel contentment by freeing your mind of the bondage that grudges produce. In your heart, you can find:

Patience *Kindness* *Truth* *Understanding* *Believe* *Hope* *Endure*

Opposites

Draw a line between the left-hand and right-hand columns connecting the humility word with its opposite. Use a thesaurus if you'd like.

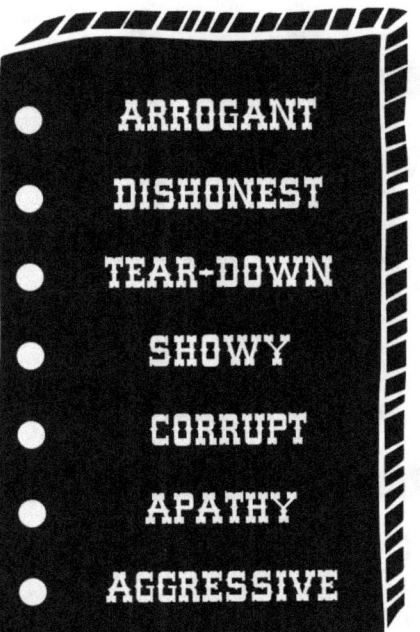

MODEST •   • ARROGANT

SELF-CONTROL •   • DISHONEST

HUMBLE •   • TEAR-DOWN

GRATITUDE •   • SHOWY

BUILD-UP •   • CORRUPT

PURE-HEARTED •   • APATHY

TRUSTWORTHY •   • AGGRESSIVE

HUMILITY MAZE

Help KIM reach the key to cultivation.
Keep track of how many keys KIM has collected on page 125....

DAY 5

Self-Esteem Or Self-Respect

The use of the words "self-esteem" and "self-respect" has become a bit muddled over the years. Though their definitions are similar, their meanings are notably different.

To esteem, something or someone is to hold them in high regard. The merit of self-esteem comes from the skills you have learned or the abilities you possess. Social media is known for this. You can show off your new outfit, dirt bike, selfie, and the like. But if everything you are is tied to a skill, an ability, or a shiny new sparkly object, you could easily fall into the trap of perfectionism—or the "look at me" syndrome. It can cause a roller coaster of emotions and keep you hooked on the online 'likes,' reactions, and comments of others.

On the other hand, self-respect is about who you *are*, not what you *have* or what you *do*. The fruits of the Spirit mentioned in *Galatians 5:22-23* ESV are also the traits of a person with self-respect: "But the fruit of the Spirit is love, joy, peace, patience, kindness, goodness, faithfulness, gentleness, and self-control; against such things, there is no law." You can gain these traits by observing and reinforcing the seven keys in this book:

WISDOM *HONOR* *HOSPITALITY* *CULTIVATION*
GENEROSITY *HUMILITY* *AUTHENTICITY*

Check the True or False box for each statement.

	T	F
Respecting yourself is a good habit.	☐	☐
Learning skills and abilities can build self-respect.	☐	☐
Self-esteem is balanced when you have self-respect.	☐	☐
A truly humble person will act like they are perfect.	☐	☐
Patient people always step to the front of the line.	☐	☐
Respectful people put others down.	☐	☐
With low self-esteem you might have self-doubt.	☐	☐

HUMILITY
Code Breaker

Use the key below to break the code.

""

BE COMPLETELY

HUMBLE AND

,

GENTLE; BE

,

PATIENT, BEARING

  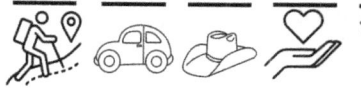 

WITH ONE ANOTHER
""

 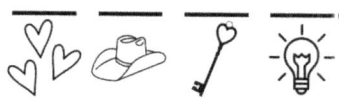.

IN LOVE.

100

DAY 6

Be Open to Constructive Criticism

Most of us don't like to show our weaknesses. What's more, we sure don't like people telling us we're wrong. But today, I want you to consider some of the great minds that have come before, like Thomas Edison. Do you think he let the criticism of others keep him from being a major influencer of ingenuity? Edison said, "I have not failed ten thousand times. I have not failed once. I have *succeeded* in proving that those ten thousand ways will not work. When I have eliminated the ways that will *not* work, I will find the way that *will* work."

Did you know that television was a failed experiment at first? It took many great minds and almost forty years before it could be a success. And did you know Albert Einstein's mistakes were many? But he was considered one of the most brilliant thinkers of our time. His theories in science are still used today. People like Edison and Einstein didn't let failure hold them back from achieving their goals. They gained success in part because they listened to what others had to contribute. Just imagine how much more educated we'd be if we listened to those that tried to guide us! *Proverbs 1:5* ESV reads, "Let the wise hear and increase in learning, and the one who understands obtain guidance." The next time someone challenges you on your thinking, pause to consider what they are saying. It just might be something that brings you to the next level of understanding.

REFLECTION TIME

How does it make you feel when your friends correct you? Angry?__ Sad?__ Thoughtful?__ Like you're not smart enough?__ Don't care?__.

How does it make you feel when you learn something difficult? Angry?__ Sad?__ Thoughtful?__ Like you're not smart enough?__ Don't care?__

How does it make you feel when you're trying hard to create something and you mess up or just can't quite get it right? Angry?__ Sad?__ Thoughtful?__ Like you're not smart enough?__ Don't care?__

Your teacher tells you to create something for the science fair that hasn't been done before. But when you create it, the project doesn't go as planned. How do you feel? Angry?__ Sad?__ Thoughtful?__ Like you're not smart enough?__ Don't care?__

HUMILITY

Self Evaluation Worksheet

Check the boxes that are true for you.

I can...	I can do this very well	I can do this fairly well	I can do this with some help	I need more practice
Consider others first				
Consider another's experiences				
Tame my tongue				
Forgive and love much				
Be open to constructive criticism				
Embrace Gratitude				

Complete the table below.

I can be humble by	
One thing I need to improve	
To improve I can	
One way I can embrace gratitude	

DAY 7

Embrace Gratitude

We have choices. We make them every day. God awakens us with brand-new mercies each morning, giving us a chance to do better than we did the day before. Gratitude goes beyond being thankful. For instance, you might be thankful for an unexpected gift, but you would be *grateful* if that gift was something you needed but couldn't afford. As another example, you may say, "thank you" when someone opens the door for you, but you would be *grateful* that you live in a community where this kind of kindness is commonly seen.

Being grateful is a way of thinking about things in a positive light. Embracing gratitude means looking for the excellence in everything and everyone. A humble person embraces gratitude because they have started their day thinking about all the things they are grateful for—and then broadcasting that goodness in their community.

I Am So Grateful

Can you name three things that you can be grateful for today? _____
_____

Name something you could do to share with another person that would brighten their day.

_____

When you think you don't have enough (of whatever it is), your 'gratitude meter' measurement goes down. Why? Because you are focusing on what you DON'T have instead of what you DO have. Take a minute to consider what you believe you are lacking...

Now, consider everything you have. Really think about it. I guarantee that the more you think about what you have, the less you will focus on what you don't have. Wise words were written by the apostle Paul in *1 Timothy 6:6-8* ESV. "But godliness with content-ment is great gain, for we brought nothing into the world, and we cannot take anything out of the world. But if we have food and clothing, with these we will be content."

HUMILITY KEY

How humble are you? Circle the best answer for each scenario.

1. It's pot luck at church today. Do you...

Hurry up to get in line first.	Let others go ahead of you in line.	Cut in line, ignoring those behind you.	Excuse yourself as you cut line to pick the items you want most.
A	B	C	D

2. A raccoon gets into the neighbor's trash. Do you...

See it and ignore it.	Walk past the trash on the ground and kick a piece of it as you walk by.	Knock on your neighbor's door and tell them about the trash.	Get a bag and go clean up the trash without telling the neighbor.
A	B	C	D

3. Your team wins the tournament. Do you...

Boast that you are the best person on the team.	Credit your success to your teammates.	Say, "We could have played better if Joe wasn't on the team."	Grab the trophy and run around the court.
A	B	C	D

4. Grandpa begins to tell you a story he's told you before. Do you...

Listen attentively, show interest, ask questions.	Interrupt Grandpa, "You've told me that story a 100 times."	Get distracted by the TV and fake interest in Grandpa's story.	Say, "I don't want to hear your stories. Thank you, anyway."
A	B	C	D

5. Your little sister makes a mess of her peanut butter and jelly sandwich. Do

Say, "Mom, she made a mess," and do nothing.	Throw away her paper plate but leave the mess.	Yell at her for making a mess.	Clean up after her without being asked.
A	B	C	D

6. You see an elderly man drop his grocery bag in the parking lot. Do you...

Figure since he's a man-he doesn't need help.	Drop your bag too so he doesn't feel bad.	Go to his aid and begin helping him pick up his groceries.	Pretend you didn't see it happen.
A	B	C	D

Talk about your answers with a parent, grandparent, or mentor.

HUMILITY
QUIZ KEY

On the Humility quiz page, you circled A, B, C or D for each scenario.

You can see below that each letter is = to a number from 0 to 3

In the 'Points' box, write the number = to the letter
you circled for each scenario in the quiz.

Next, add the numbers together at the bottom for your total.

1. A=0 B=3 C=1 D=2

2. A=0 B=1 C=2 D=3

3. A=1 B=3 C=0 D=2

4. A=3 B=0 C=1 D=2

5. A=1 B=2 C=0 D=3

6. A=2 B=1 C=3 D=0

Points

+ _____

Next, write your total from this page in the Humility
box on page 123 to calculate your overall score.

Total

Dad and me in our living room, Christmas 1974

" Could a greater miracle take place than for us to look through each other's eyes for an instant? "

Henry David Thoreau

AUTHENTICITY

Sing Me Back Home

It was nearing Dad's final day in his earthly body. The glioblastoma from cancer had taken his voice and most of his physical and mental sharpness. On that particular night, a few of our family members gathered around Dad's bed. My brother, Brandt, and one of Dad's brothers, Uncle David, had flown in for a visit. My mom and I were also there that night. There was a constant ache within our family unit as we were painfully aware Dad's days were growing short.

Dad loved singing and strumming songs on his guitar—and occasionally the fiddle. Before he got too sick, he performed weekly with his brother, Doyar, at the Jimmy Driftwood Barn, a small venue in the Ozarks of Arkansas. Family get-togethers usually found us gathered around in a circle of sorts—pickin', grinnin', and tapping our toes to the music weaving the backdrop of my life.

One of the songs Dad used to sing was a 1960s song about a jailed man on death row, convicted of a crime for which he would lose his life. The words "Sing Me Back Home" echoed through my soul that night with the striking and eerily similar lyrics of my dad's own 'prison' from cancer. Dad's desire, though unspoken, was to hear music again before he went home to his Heavenly Father.

The night was solemn as we gathered around Dad's bed. Our voices were low to allow him to rest. My brother had the guitar on his lap, gently strumming chords, unable to find a song he'd have the emotional strength to play and sing. Dad had taught Brandt to play when he was young. I tried to encourage my brother with some tunes I knew he could play. We started with 'Take Me Home, Country Roads' by John Denver—A song I'd sung with Dad many times over the years.

Dad lay in bed with his eyes closed, listening to the songs we all sang as my brother strummed along. We continued with other favorites from artists like Merle Haggard and Marty Robbins— and hymns like the timeless classics, 'Amazing Grace' and 'How Great Thou Art.' Although the lumps in our throats were keeping the beautiful melodies from coming through as we intended, I know it brought joy to Dad's heart to hear them once again.

While I was growing up, prayer wasn't the norm in our home. Because of Dad's soured church experience during his early years, he decided formal church was not for him. Nonetheless, God's plan for our family was one of prosperity rather than harm. He gave us a journey of hope —and a future with abundant blessings. With that new perspective, Dad started going back to church. The ripple effect of his influence expanded dramatically through his gift of serving others.

That night, as my family continued singing in melancholic voices, I knew it would become a cherished memory. We decided to call it a night as it was getting quite late. But first, we all held hands together with Dad. Then, Uncle David led us in prayer at Dad's side. We each took turns praying, feeling thanks to our merciful God for allowing us this precious time with Dad . . . and for blessing us with a family full of love and unity.

After we had all taken our turns and started to loosen our handhold, we all heard quiet utterances coming from Dad's mouth while he was still gripping our hands. We looked up to see a peaceful smile on his face. HE WAS PRAYING! Dad had brought our hearts together again, rejoining us in prayer as he spoke his words to the Lord. We could not comprehend his words, but we knew Dad's heart. We knew he loved the Lord and was confessing those truths. There was not a dry eye in the room. We closed in prayer with a unanimous "Amen" when Dad's prayer ended. Our hearts were overjoyed to hear him pray out loud one more time.

Dad's authenticity shone through that heavy-hearted night with such brilliance. His peace illuminated the somber room. Even in the most challenging moments of his life, his heart was centered on worshipping and communicating with the One who loved him most.

DAY 1

Authenticity is a Choice

You make judgment calls every day: What you wear, how you act toward your family members, whether you are joyful, angry, calm, or stressed. Every emotion is a choice. When you wake up in the morning and first open your eyes, determine how your day will go. Putting your thoughts in order before you place your feet on the floor will help your day be more thoughtful rather than reactionary.

I admit that not all days will be good days. Life has a way of throwing us unexpected and unavoidable situations. But, in each of these, we have the choice of how we will handle it. We each react uniquely, depending on our thought processes. The idea here is to consciously decide that whatever you do, say, or think will be a positive flow from your truest self.

Let me give an example. Your brother bumps into you as he walks past you. Whether or not he bumped into you intentionally, your reaction might be frustration or anger. However, if you take just a few seconds to collect your thoughts about the incident, you can simply let it go or address the matter calmly. Maybe your sibling meant to be mean, or perhaps they just weren't paying attention. Either way, it's your choice how you will handle the situation. Words to follow in *1 John 3:18 NLT*: "Dear children, let's not merely say that we love each other; let us show the truth by our actions."

> "Attitude is a choice. Happiness is a choice. Optimism is a choice.
> Kindness is a choice. Giving is a choice. Respect is a choice.
> Whatever choice you make makes you. Choose wisely."
> Roy T. Bennett, in *The Light in the Heart*

DAY 2

Sing Your Song

Do you like to sing out loud? In the shower? Around family only? In a crowd? Music has a way of sinking into our bones, touching us in a very different way than just communicating by talking. You know the feeling when your favorite jam is played. It might make you want to get up and dance—or put you in a certain mood. Do you play an instrument? Even instrumental music can awaken a different part of our brains.

In the story, 'Sing Me Back Home,' Dad developed a brain tumor that limited his ability to sing and play his instruments. But even this major setback did not keep him from singing his song in his own way when he added to the prayer that night. *Psalms 108:1* ESV reads, "My heart is steadfast, O God! I will sing and make melody with all my being!" With all honesty, I can say that Dad had the heart of a steadfast servant to the last.

That's the cool thing about authenticity. It's yours and yours alone. The melody of every song is a little different, and so are we. God created each of us to sing our own song, not someone else's. So, this is your time to shine. Right now, determine the type of person you will become. God gave us each a brilliant mind. He also gave us a choice to use our minds any way we want. Make the exceptional choice to be the best version of your authentic self you can be.

Turn This Scene Around

Your friend bailed out on movie night, saying she was sick. Through another friend, you found out she was lying. She had just made an excuse. You have all kinds of thoughts running through your head, including how you'd like to text her something mean-spirited or never talk to her again.

Now, when I snap my finger, you have come up with a brilliant solution to extend genuine love to her. How would you show her your best self? Explain below. Ready...and...

_____

_____

_____

AUTHENTICITY SCRAMBLE

Unscramble the words in the first row by connecting them with their match on the right.

RIFA • • PURPOSEFUL

NEPTECOIPR • • CREDIBLE

ROECAGU • • FAIR

CIRSENE • • PERCEPTION

DIBEECLR • • SINCERE

SOPEFUULPR • • MINDFUL

FLIDMUN • • COURAGE

DAY 3

Perception

Have you ever been to a carnival and walked through a house of mirrors? Yes__ or No__ If yes, was it scary, mind-blowing, or ridiculous? _____ One thing is for sure. It plays tricks on your mind.

I remember being nervous the first time I went through a house of mirrors, unsure of what I might find. Pulling back the curtain to go inside, I suddenly faced a completely distorted image of myself. It looked like my head had shrunk to the shape of a small pear, but my belly and legs were shaped like tall and slender green beans. In each mirror that I saw, my figure appeared distorted beyond belief. I looked like the letter "S" in one mirror and a cone head in another. There was a mini-me, a giant me, and even one where I was cloned and infinitely replicated. There were many versions of ME.

What do you see in a regular mirror with no distortion? Is the image an accurate view of yourself? What you perceive about yourself affects how you make every decision. You are tapping into your authentic self when you become aware of this. Have you ever heard the saying, "You are what you *think* you are?" *Proverbs 4:23* of the NLT reads, "Guard your heart above all else, for it determines the course of your life."

The age you are now is one of the most challenging. With the changes you are going through at this time, sometimes your emotions are all over the place. Please be sure to give yourself grace. This turmoil will pass. You are also making decisions that sometimes might seem like a tug-of-war with your parents. I assure you that it's all part of being human and growing to your full potential. Just remember to be respectful during these times. Develop smart communication skills. The one thing you want to avoid is comparing yourself to others. Everyone has an individual journey they experience with their unique strengths. Comparison is a thief. It makes you think that what you have to offer isn't good enough. Ignore this dangerous mindset. Take on the perspective of believing in yourself and embracing your originality!

- Name three things you like about yourself. _____
  _____
- Name three things you want to improve about yourself. _____
  _____
- Do you behave differently around friends than you do family? _____
  _____
- What is one special trait about you that is different than your friends? _____
  _____
- Do you think it's important that your friends know the true you? _____ Why or why not?
  _____

AUTHENTICITY

WORD SEARCH

```
C  R  A  E  L  B  A  H  C  A  E  T
T  H  O  U  G  H  T  F  U  L  T  X
D  R  A  C  H  I  W  A  S  T  A  M
G  E  N  U  I  N  E  S  D  W  C  B
E  R  T  E  T  A  E  R  R  W  I  I
T  X  C  V  U  H  E  P  Y  I  N  A
R  Z  A  S  R  D  E  W  E  O  U  B
E  Q  W  E  I  N  O  N  P  W  M  H
A  M  V  S  N  V  C  E  T  R  M  Z
L  E  N  A  N  B  C  X  A  I  O  W
B  O  H  E  L  P  F  U  L  E  C  Q
C  Y  H  T  R  O  W  T  S  U  R  T
P  I  R  Q  E  A  S  I  V  N  M  B
```

TEACHABLE	COMMUNICATE	AUTHENTIC
THOUGHTFUL	HELPFUL	GET REAL
TRUSTWORTHY	GENUINE	CONSIDER

DAY 4
Recognize Failures As Growth

Let's face it: Failure is part of life. But are we meant to give up after one, two, or three failures? Absolutely not. Why? Because we mature when we learn from our mistakes. Years ago, my younger cousin, Tad, asked me if I could change anything about my life, what would it be? That question made me pause. Then I said, "You know, Tad, I don't think I'd change a thing —because the experiences I had along the way made me the person I am today. I'm stronger for having gone through them."

You can't avoid making mistakes. And that's okay. What you choose to do with the knowledge you gained from your failures is where real growth can happen. And you're in good company! The greatest minds and inventors of our times are among those who have failed the most. Yet, they didn't give up! They accepted their failures as growth, making explosive progress in ingenuity and technology.

You might say that failure doesn't make sense. But how will you know success if you're unwilling to challenge your mind after a few failures? Can you ever predict what you could accomplish if you don't try? And that's not all. When others see you're trying, they, in turn, will be inspired. You—Yes, YOU—are capable of the same type of extraordinary accomplishments as our forefathers.

Opposites

Draw a line between the left-hand and right-hand columns connecting the authenticity word with its opposite. Use a thesaurus if you'd like.

GENUINE

LEGIT

MINDFUL

CREDIBLE

STEADFAST

APPRECIATE

INCORRUPTIBLE

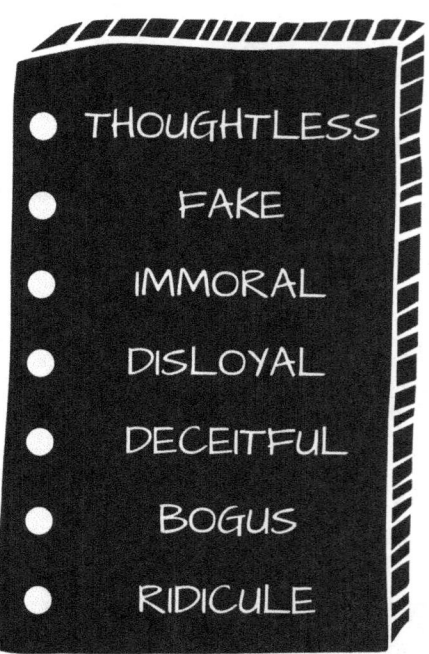

THOUGHTLESS

FAKE

IMMORAL

DISLOYAL

DECEITFUL

BOGUS

RIDICULE

AUTHENTICITY MAZE

Help KIM reach the key to cultivation.
Keep track of how many keys KIM has collected on page 125....

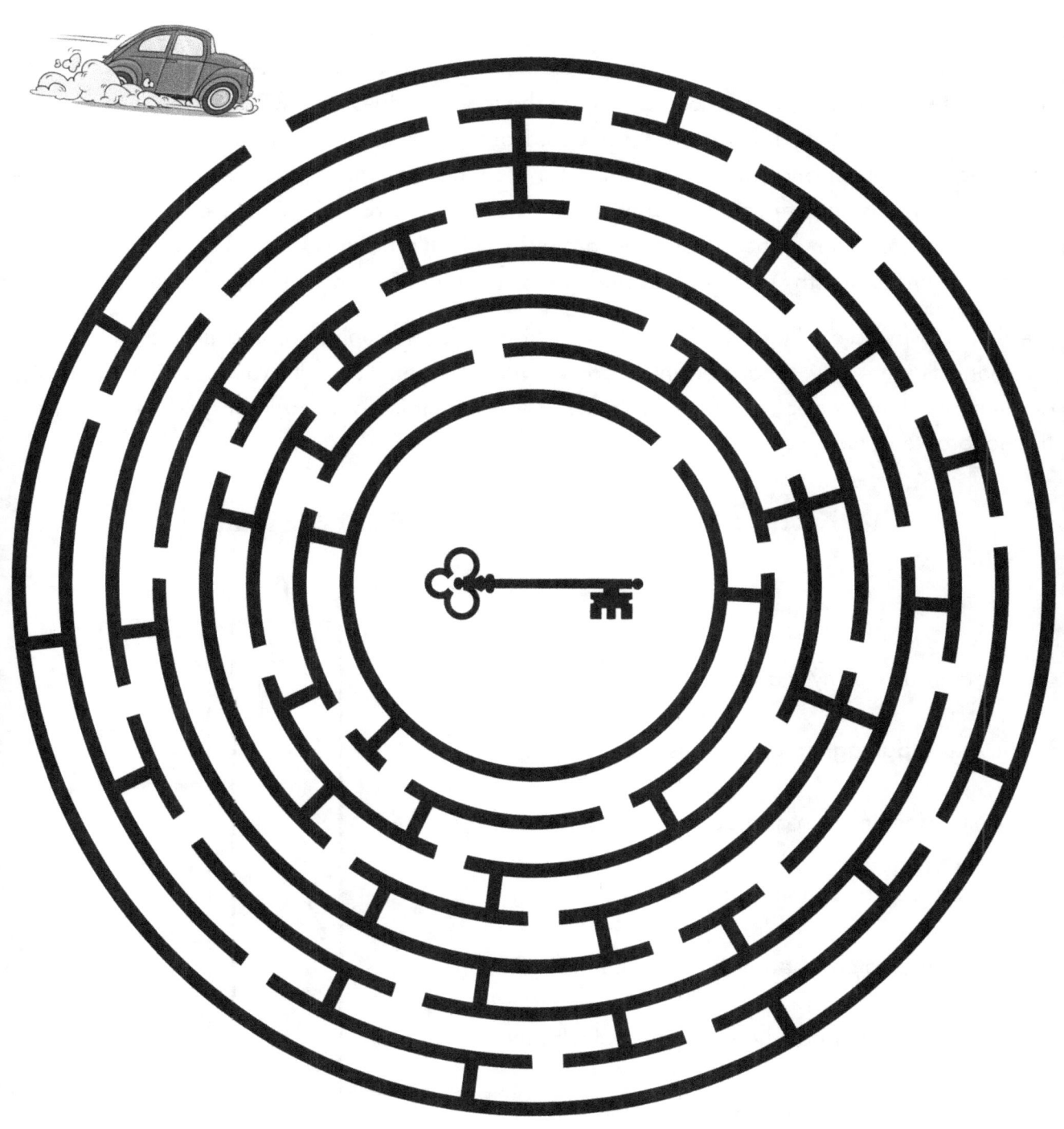

DAY 5
Honesty Is The Best Policy

The saying, "Honesty is the best policy," is centuries old. That tells me something. It is not just some trendy comment. This saying has survived through the centuries because it is a true statement. And in the end, the truth will always be better than lies.

Do you struggle in this area? To be fair, we have all been challenged with honesty at one time or another. It may seem like dishonest people get away with their lies. But do they *really*? In the short term, it may appear that way. But in the long run, they don't. God knows every detail about us, down to the last hair on our heads. Doesn't it make sense that he is aware of the times we are honest and the times we lie? So then, do we want to be honest only to please God? Well, pleasing Him should definitely be a motivator. But we should also be drawn to making decisions that benefit everyone around us. That's because we want to do the right thing to promote healthy relationships and communication: Forging a bond of trust.

Stephen Covey said, "Moral authority comes from following universal and timeless principles like honesty, integrity, and treating people with respect." So, do you see how honesty, authenticity, and respect go hand in hand? These principles are the light guiding us toward the honorable person we strive to become.

Check the True or False box for each statement.

	T	F
Being trustworthy is a weakness.	☐	☐
Lies are damaging to relationships.	☐	☐
Being genuine can also be fake.	☐	☐
Failure can be a time of growth.	☐	☐
It is your choice whether to be authentic or not.	☐	☐
People appreciate when you are real with them.	☐	☐
Truth and rumor are always the same thing.	☐	☐

DAY 6

Practice Mindfulness

Breathing . . . It's not something we typically think about unless we have something like a stuffy nose, asthma, or get winded playing a sport. But breathing is essential to life.

Have you ever heard of mindfulness? Maybe you practice it in school as a way to calm the class. Simply put, mindfulness is being aware of your thoughts. Breathing is used to center your thoughts in this practice. It relaxes your whole body. During this time, you breathe and empty your mind of your stressors. People also use controlled breathing strategies during prayer and meditation. It's a great time to invite the Holy Spirit into your prayer time because it helps you focus.

Controlled breathing is an excellent practice to start if you don't already do it. The list of benefits is long, and they multiply if the method is used regularly. Besides increasing awareness, some benefits include reducing stress levels, clarifying a situation, and reminding you to be yourself. It's a technique you can use throughout your life and only takes a few minutes a day. You can find many such strategies online. Ask a parent to guide you to the one that works best for you. Here's a simple one anyone can do:

Find a quiet area to sit upright in a comfortable position. With one hand on your belly, take three deep breaths—in through your nose and out through your mouth. Continue the deep breathing as you feel your belly rise and fall. Be aware that your mind will probably drift. Recenter your thinking back to the rise and fall of your belly. Do this for three to five minutes a day, whether or not you're stressed. You will feel the benefits in no time.

 **REFLECTION TIME**

How do you feel when you see people fight? Angry?__ Sad?__ Scared?__
Doesn't bother me?__ Don't care?__

How does it make you feel when you are trying to study and another is making need-less noise? Angry?__ Sad?__ Scared?__ Doesn't bother me?__ Don't care?__

How does it make you feel when you are accused of lying but are innocent? Angry?__ Sad?__
Scared?__ Doesn't both me?__ Don't care?__

How does it make you feel to fail a test in school? Angry?__ Sad?__ Scared?__
Doesn't bother me?__ Don't care?__

Consider your answers above. Next time you face a difficult challenge, try practicing the mindfulness technique. In what ways might it help you? _____

_____

AUTHENTICITY Code Breaker

Use the key below to break the code.

A	B	C	D	E	F	G	H	I	J	K	L	M

N	O	P	Q	R	S	T	U	V	W	X	Y	Z

"When she speaks her words are,"

"her words are"

"wise, and she gives"

"instructions"

"with kindness."

> "When she speaks, her words are wise, and she gives instructions with kindness."

AUTHENTICITY

Self Evaluation Worksheet

Check the boxes that are true for you.

I can...	I can do this very well	I can do this fairly well	I can do this with some help	I need more practice
Choose to be authentic				
Sing my song				
Perceive myself accurately				
Recognize my failures as growth				
Practice mindfulness				
Keep it real				

Complete the table below.

I can be authentic by	
One thing I need to improve	
To improve I can	
One failure that I've learned from	

DAY 7

Keep It Real

"Keeping it real" embraces three vital concepts to live by:

1 Hold firm to choosing to be respectful every time. To guide you, use the seven keys you've learned in this book: *Wisdom, honor, hospitality, cultivation, generosity, humility, and authenticity.*

2 Be vulnerable enough to be humble and open-hearted-but strong enough to walk away from toxic relationships.

3 Embrace the fact that you're unique, with special God-given talents that only *you* can give to the world.

Through it all, don't forget to be yourself! You will find your tribe and connections. That loving community will also bring you the most joy because you won't have to be someone you're not—just to fit in.

Write three things about you that are real. _____

_____

Name something you are prideful about owning (For example: designer shoes, jewelry, or a cell phone). _____ Did you get this item in order to gain status among your friends? If so, does this item define the type of person you want to become? ____ If you didn't get it as an object of status, are you boastful or arrogant about owning it? ___ If you didn't have this item but wanted it, would it change how you felt about others who *did* have it? ___ How so? _____ We have definite needs like food, water, shelter, and clothing. It is not necessary to own every trendy item. Balance is key for needs and wants.

It's possible for adolescents to lose their God-given identity if they're making poor choices during these challenging years of their lives. So, write the name of a good friend, parent, guardian, or mentor that you will turn to when you need to recenter your values and beliefs.

120

AUTHENTICITY KEY

How authentic are you? Circle the best answer for each scenario.

1. Your mentor took the time to teach you something valuable. Do you...

Tell your mentor she doesn't know what she's talking about.	Think what she taught you is unimportant.	Walk away and forget what you were taught.	Thank her for her time and seriously consider what she taught you.
A	B	C	D

2. You shake your buddy's hand to seal the deal when you agree to buy his bike. Do you...

Agree to pay for it next week, then follow through with the $$.	Blow it off because you don't want it after all and fail to let him know.	Bring him 1/2 the $$ and try to get the bike 1/2 the agreed price.	Steal the bike and think, "He's my friend. He won't get mad."
A	B	C	D

3. Your friend is going through a really difficult time. Do you...

Tell her to get over it.	Ignore her phone calls.	Carefully listen to your friend and help the best way you know how.	Not know what to say, so you don't say anything at all.
A	B	C	D

4. A friend of the family just passed away. Do you...

Express genuine sympathy to your friend's family members.	Say and do nothing because you don't know what to say.	Think, "I can't be around a bunch of sad people."	Show no concern whatsoever.
A	B	C	D

5. You have a gut feeling something bad is about to go down. Do you...

Join in because you love the idea of danger.	Consider the possibility of danger and decide not to participate.	Consider you haven't been grounded lately, so you go for it.	Go along but pray you don't get in trouble.
A	B	C	D

6. Your grandma tells you to make wise choices. Do you...

Throw caution to the wind—I'll deal with the consequences.	Say, "I'd rather be foolish, but thank you."	Tell your Grandma, "I don't want my friends to think I'm a goody-goody."	Consider your ways and decide to be your best self and make good choices.
A	B	C	D

Talk about your answers with a parent, grandparent, or mentor.

AUTHENTICITY
QUIZ KEY

On the Authenticity quiz page, you circled A, B, C or D for each scenario.

You can see below that each letter is = to a number from 0 to 3

In the 'Points' box, write the number = to the letter
you circled for each scenario in the quiz.

Next, add the numbers together at the bottom for your total.

1. A=0 B=2 C=1 D=3

2. A=3 B=1 C=2 D=0

3. A=0 B=1 C=3 D=2

4. A=3 B=2 C=1 D=0

5. A=0 B=3 C=2 D=1

6. A=0 B=1 C=2 D=3

Points

+ _____

Next, write your total from this page in the
Authenticity box on page 123 to calculate your
overall score.

Total

GRAND FINALE

How did you do?

Wisdom ☐

Honor ☐

Hospitality ☐

Cultivation ☐

Generosity ☐

Humility ☐

Authenticity ☐

Total Score

☐

If you scored 85-126

ADVANCED

You have mastered the keys. Well done. You are a quiz whiz. Your ripple effect will grow as you continue to master these keys in your everyday life. Way to go! Now, invite a friend to take this quiz.

If you scored 43-84

EMERGING

You are developing your keys to respect, but you need some improvement. Go back to the scenarios where you could have chosen a better answer. Consider ways you can improve your character in these areas. You'll get there.

If you scored 0-42

NOVICE

Looks like you need some work in the respect department. But! All is not lost. You need to unlock your respect potential. Go back through the stories and lessons, looking for key points that you can practice every day. Choose to be respectful in everything you do.

May your words be seasoned with thoughtfulness and your life journey be 'kindness in motion'.

ANSWER KEYS

WORD SCRAMBLES

WISDOM

veersbo, observe; stilen, listen; cuedeta, educate; cviead, advice; lerftec, reflect; utthr, truth; wedngleko, knowledge.

HONOR

tabueerpl, reputable; lomar, moral; yonsteh, honesty; plcinirep, principle; tevecobij, objective; sulpecetfr, respectful; gettiyrin, integrity.

HOSPITALITY

picsoomans, compassion; dangidnusertn, understanding; nitaetont, attention; yescurot, courtesy; sowheflipl, fellowship; teggrine, greeting; teadersinco, considerate.

CULTIVATION

stisas, assist; flupit, uplift; erturnu, nurture; opsutrp, support; lceenuogar, encourage; golliwod, goodwill; hipstonireal, relationship.

GENEROSITY

muflcrei merciful; sgodnesco, goodness; elupfhl, helpful; refof, offer; vleo, love; rahes, share; bdantuna, abundant.

HUMILITY

tapenit, patient; futidul, dutiful; vedreres, reserved; tenpresuoitun, unpretentious; deotibne, obedient; smeksnee, meekness; sanumsignu, unassuming.

AUTHENTICITY

rifa, fair; neptecoipr, perception; roecagu, courage; cirsene, sincere; dibeeclr, credible; sopefuulpr, purposeful; flidmun, mindful.

WORD SEARCHES

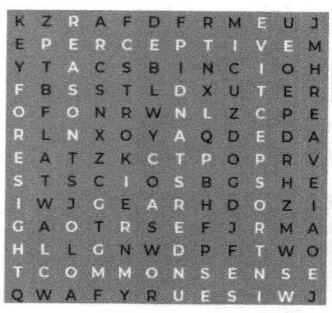
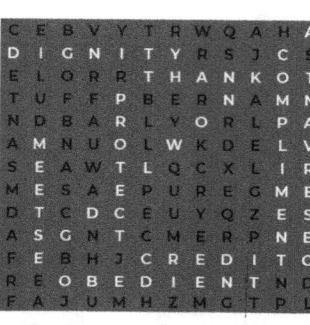
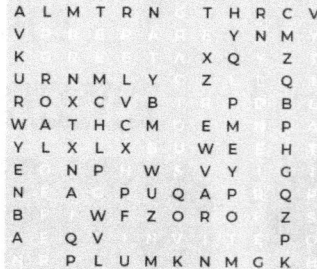

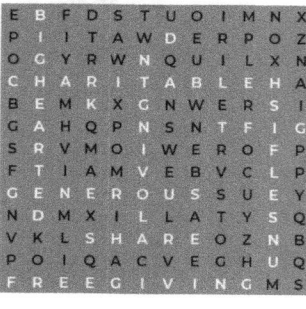

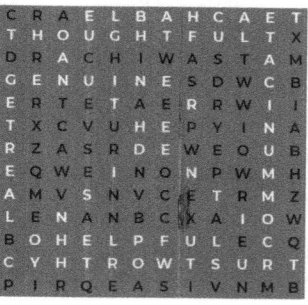

OPPOSITES

WISDOM
Guide, mislead; know, misunderstand; learn, forget; sense, foolishness; curiosity, disinterest; alert, careless; level-headed, angst.

HONOR
Listen, ignore; compliment, criticize; fair, unjust; loyal, unfaithful; integrity, disrespect; upright, corrupt; admirable, dispicable.

HOSPITALITY
Invite, exclude; entertain, neglect; polite, rude; generous, scrooge-like; prepared, unready; social, anti-social; welcoming, unreceptive.

CULTIVATION
Inspire, dishearten; active, stalled; unite, abandon; develop, tear-down; gather, separate; lead, follow; confident, uncertain.

GENEROSITY
Gentle, harsh; selfless, self-seeking; charitable, merciless; thoughtful, inconsiderate; offer, refusal; plentiful, lacking; give, take.

HUMILITY
Modest, showy; self-control, aggressive; humble, arrogant; gratitude, apathy; build-up, tear-down; pure-hearted-corrupt; trust-worthy, dishonest.

AUTHENTICITY
Genuine, fake; legit, bogus; mindful, thoughtless; credible, deceitful; steadfast, disloyal; appreciate, ridicule; incorruptible, immoral.

MAZES

Color each key as KIM collects them from the mazes.

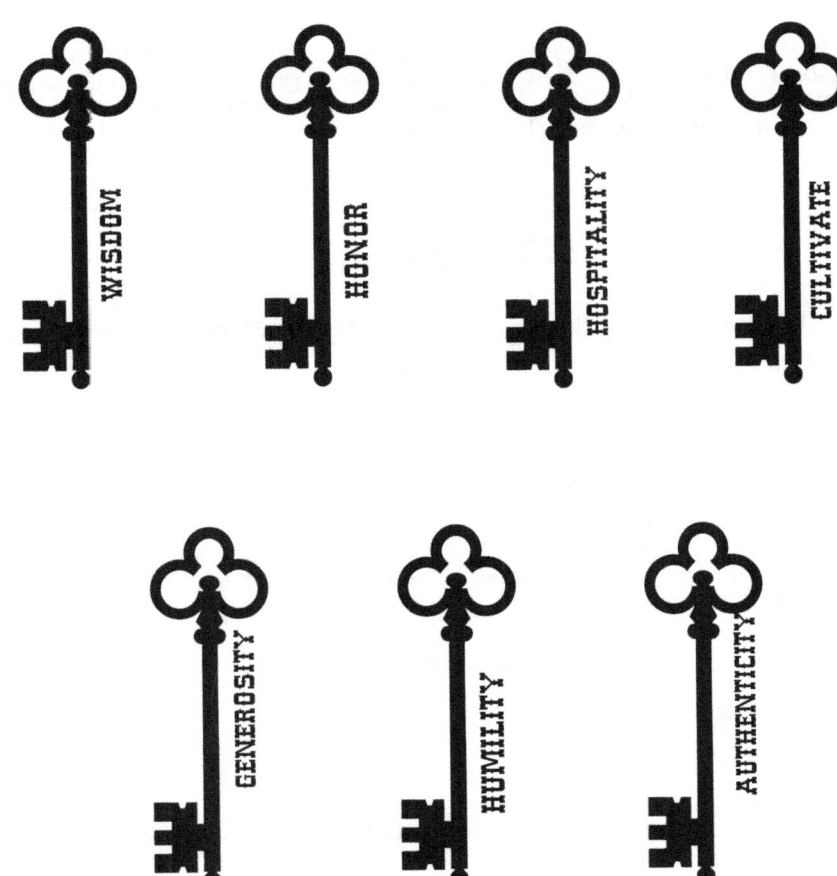

TRUE & FALSE

WISDOM Asking advice is for the weak-minded. [False] Wisdom is developed over time. [True] Wisdom is foolishness. [False] A desire to learn assures you won't be easily bored. [True] Ignoring a wise person is thoughtless. [True] Knowledge is a powerful tool. [True] You have all the wisdom you need at the age of 18. [False]

HONOR Kindness is weakness. [False] You should always have the first say in a conversation. [False] Honor is a strength. [True] Doing the right thing is a good thing. [True] Conversations are best when you're angry. [False] Ignoring the needs of others is helpful. [False] Listening builds better relationships. [True]

HOSPITALITY Starting a conversation can make your guest at ease. [True] Cordial means warm and sincere. [True] It is polite to take your friend's earbuds without asking. [False] When you serve others, it is a kindness. [True] Treat your guest like you'd want to be treated. [True] Being rude to others is highly advised. [False] Ignoring your friend builds a better relationship. [False]

CULTIVATION God is a gentle guide and strong protector. [True] Your journey is easier with God in the pilot's seat. [True] It's good to lead your friends into risky situations. [False] Selfish ways will surely make God happy. [False] Embracing meanness will cause you trouble. [True] Cultivating relationships will help you earn respect. [True] You will be more confident if you have self-respect. [True]

GENEROSITY Generosity means self-seeking. [False] A smile could lift someone's sadness. [True] Kindness is a strength. [True] Doing things without obligation is a good thing. [True] To give and expect something in return is advised. [False] There are countless ways to pay it forward. [True] It is more blessed to give than receive. [True]

HUMILITY Respecting yourself is a good habit. [True] Learning skills and abilities can build self-respect. [True] Self-esteem is balanced when you have self-respect. [True] A truly humble person will act like they are perfect. [False] Patient people always step to the front of the line. [False] Respectful people put others down. [False] With low self-esteem you might have self-doubt. [True]

AUTHENTICITY Being trustworthy is a weakness. [False] Lies are damaging to relationships. [True] Being genuine can also be fake. [False] Failure can be a time of growth. [True] It is your choice whether to be authentic or not. [True] People appreciate when you are real with them. [True] Truth and rumor are always the same the same thing. [False]

CODE BREAKERS

WISDOM "How much better to get wisdom than gold, to get insight rather than silver." Proverbs 16:16 NIV

HONOR "Whoever pursues righteousness and love finds life, properity, and honor." Proverbs 21:21 NIV

HOSPITALITY "And do not neglect doing good and sharing, for with such scrifices God is pleased." Hebrews 13:16 NASB

CULTIVATION "Above all, love each other deeply, because love covers over a multitude of sins." 1 Peter 4:8 NIV

GENEROSITY "For where your treasure is, there your heart will be also." Matthew 6:21 ESV

HUMILITY "Be completely humble and gentle; be patient, bearing with one another in love." Ephesians 4:2 NIV

AUTHENTICITY "When she speaks, her words are wise and she gives instructions with kindness." Proverbs 31:26 NIV